THE PROFOUND PHILOSOPHICAL PONTIFICATIONS OF BIG JOHN DEACON

Freemason Extraordinaire

Volume IV

JAMES "CHRIS" WILLIAMS IV

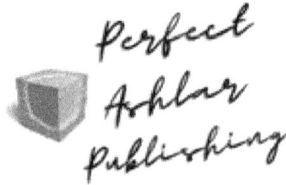

Perfect Ashlar Publishing

Universal City, TX

For ordering information please visit Perfect Ashlar Publishing's website at:
www.PerfectAshlarPublishing.com

DEDICATION

To my Brothers of Davy Crockett Lodge, who supported and encouraged me to keep writing, especially, Brother Brad Kohanke and his wife, Crystal and Brother Burt Reynolds and his wife Ana, who compiled the first two years of my stories and presented them to me in book form, which showed me that this book series was possible.

To William A. Smith for assisting my Brothers in that early project.

This book is dedicated to my family: JC, Tiff, Sarah, Megan, Travis, Chandler, and Jordan; along with all my other unofficial proofreaders. I cannot express enough how important you all were.

To all my Masonic Brothers who do what Masons do, have provided the story lines and situations in the John Deacon series. Thank you all for being my Brothers! I hope somehow Brother John has both entertained and educated you. If so, I have accomplished my purpose.

To my Dad, James C. Williams III, the ultimate and authentic cowboy, and my Mom Billye, thank you both for a lifetime of ideas and inspiration.

And finally, to my wife Pam, who makes my life what it is. Without her support, none of this could have happened.

TABLE OF CONTENTS

FORWARD

My first encounter with Brother Chris Williams was at the Texas Wardens Retreat in Corpus Christi, Texas. As a reasonably new Master Mason who was drafted into serving his Lodge as an officer, I was overwhelmed. But Brother Chris eased my nerves with his insightful guidance on proper lodge operations and unique storytelling to fill in the gaps to help me see the big picture. Much of what I learned from Brother Chris and the other members of the Education Committee helped shape my Masonic leadership philosophy leading to a very successful year as Worshipful Master of my Lodge.

Fast forward a few years, and while having a conversation with Brother Chris, he shared with me the Big John Deacon stories that he wrote for the Davy Crockett Newsletter. I was honored that he would ask me to publish these stories for all of you to read. While preparing the four-volume set for publication, I laughed, cried, and was inspired by Brother John Deacon's antics and profound philosophy.

I firmly believe that the four John Deacon books have solidified Brother Chris Williams' legacy as a great Mason. Brother Chris has impacted so many with his friendship and Brotherly Love, and readers for years to come will now get to experience that same warmth inside the pages of each John Deacon Book. That truly is a legacy to admire and celebrate!

Christophor J. Galloway,

Past Mast of Valley-Hi Lodge #1407 &

Author of Leading from the East:

Innovative Strategies for Masonic Lodges

THE COUNTY LINE. Legendary Bar-B-Q

Masonic Wisdom At The County Line

I know that I complain about Big John Deacon all the time, and it may seem like I dread meeting with him every month. But that is not true. Yes, he is a financial drain on my pocketbook, but I have to admit that he has taught me a lot. No, he hasn't sat me down schoolroom style and proceeded to teach me things about Masonry. Instead, it has been an experience-based learning program. You know, just the experience of spending time with him and soaking up the things he has to say and then applying those things to myself and my situation. Sometimes, no, a lot of times, he seems to straddle the line between the twilight zone and the outer limits. Those of you who read his words regularly know what I mean. But there are those times, too, where there is clarity through all the weirdness and craziness. He has taught me more about myself than I ever imagined, and therein lies the reason why I keep paying for his lunch. Thank God it's only once a month!

This month I was looking forward to seeing him because I had something to talk to him about. John called me and told me that he was sitting at a restaurant at the County Line. It only took a second for the confusion to clear and inform him that he was not sitting near the county line but was at the County Line Restaurant.

"Whatever," was the growled response. "You had better get here quick before I eat more than you can pay for." I flatly informed him that I was definitely not buying his lunch this time and then realized I was talking to a deadline. I don't know why I never thought of the County Line for one of our lunches, but I was looking forward to it since I hadn't been there for that good BBQ for a while. It took me about 20 minutes to get there, and as I walked in the door, I could hear his laughter coming from somewhere towards the rear of the room. John had his back to me. As I approached the table, I noticed he had what looked like four different appetizers placed in a semi-circle in front of him. There was something called Mexican Deviled Eggs which looked awesome; there were some fried cheese bites with ranch dressing to dip them in, a bowl of queso and chips was there along with some BBQ Brisket sliders. Man, there was enough food there for several people, and any thoughts I may have had about sampling any of it quickly faded away as John slid each plate closer to him as I sat down.

I found out he was laughing because our server had suggested that there might be a few more people joining him for lunch. I began looking over the menu as he resumed his appetizers. Our server Sally brought me an iced tea and asked me for my order. I ordered the BBQ sausage sandwich, which I remembered was delicious along with fried okra and green beans. She smiled and turned towards the kitchen only to hear John loudly clearing his throat.

"Hey, Darlin," he said as she turned to him with a confused look on her face. Considering the amount of food already consumed by the big guy, she incorrectly assumed that he was done ordering. She glanced at me with a half-smile, arching her eyebrows towards John. I just shrugged my shoulders as he ordered, not surprisingly, a giant Chicken Fried Steak and a plate of pork ribs with all the usual side orders, of course. Sally headed for the kitchen shaking her head in disbelief as they all do, and I waited for him to finish his pre-lunch lunch.

I wanted to ask him something I had been thinking about for a few weeks so John could mull it over while he ate.... or continued to eat. But it was not to be because just as he pushed the last plate of snacks away, Sally appeared with our actual lunch. I watched him survey all he had ordered and suggested that he might want to walk around a little bit before starting in on the spread that Sally sat in front of him. John looked at me like I was crazy. I am sure his only thought was that I or someone might deprive him of even one morsel of his lunch. There was nothing to do then but eat, so I concentrated on my Sausage sandwich, and as usual, I finished before him. It wasn't long before he finished, and as Sally cleared the last plate from in front of him, I said, "I need to bounce something off of you, John."

John got a weird expression on his face, and I braced myself for the sarcasm but instead, his reply was, "Bounce away, my Brother."

"Well, I need to get the opinion of a wise and learned Brother about a certain issue," I began. I could see the satisfied expression in his eyes that I considered him wise and learned as I continued. "But since you are here, I will just ask you instead." (The satisfied expression disappeared in an instant).

"I'm just kidding, John. You are the perfect Brother to speak to about this. I have been involved for a couple of months in an ongoing discussion with a few Brothers about opening an Entered Apprentice Lodge to allow the Entered Apprentices to attend and become part of the Lodge family as soon as they are made Masons. We have debated whether it has done anything to stop the loss of our new EA's. I have even been presented with figures from Grand Lodge reports showing that the law change has done nothing to slow down the number of our new Entered Apprentices from not finishing their work and continuing their Masonic journey. In fact, according to the numbers, the problem has worsened. Now I am starting to wonder if changing the law was even worth it."

I stopped and waited for him to say something, anything, but he just sat there staring at me, and his expression went from neutral to puzzled and then to disbelief. I began to wonder what the heck was going on inside his mind. It should have been working ok since I had waited until he finished his lunch. He began to slowly shake his head. I threw up my hands, exasperated, to shake his head slowly. "Are you going to say something or what?"

"What I have to say, Brother Chris," he said evenly. "Is what you already know or should know. First of all, the opening of a Lodge in the EA Degree for the benefit of new EAs, while necessary, is only one piece of the whole puzzle, but I will come back to that in a minute. Since we are talking about facts and figures, to prove a point, let's start with the fact that very few Lodges in our Grand jurisdiction have taken advantage of the law change and are opening their Lodge in the EA Degree. They simply refuse to do so. To make the numbers correct, you would need to account only for the Lodges that *DO* open in an EA Lodge; otherwise, the result is skewed. Out of the 80,000 some odd Brothers in our Grand Jurisdiction, there are less than 1,000 total esoteric teaching certificate holders. That is less than one per Lodge. Not to mention that there is little to no Masonic Education of any kind going on in the majority of our Lodges at this time. Now tell me, Brother Chris, how many new Entered Apprentices has your Lodge had in the last 12 months? And how many have you lost?"

I didn't have to think hard on that one, so I quickly answered, "We have had 24 total, John, and of that total, ten have been raised to the sublime degree of a Master Mason. Five are still working on their Fellow

Craft work, and there are eight still working on their Entered Apprentice work. Sadly, there is one that seems to have decided not to continue."

"That's pretty darn good, Brother Chris," he replied with a smile. Those stats sound a little like my Lodge too. So since I know that you open Lodge in the Entered Apprentice Degree for your Stated Meetings, how many of them attend Lodge meetings."

The answer to that question made me smile as it does all the Brothers of our Lodge. I proudly said, "We usually see between seven and twelve Entered Apprentices and Fellow Crafts at our meetings, and it's not always the same ones. Add that to our regular Brother's attendance, and we have between 25 and 40 Brothers at our Stated Meetings."

John was nodding now as I talked and then said, "It must be hard to find instructors for all of those candidates, and assigning a mentor is surely out of the question, isn't it?"

I finally figured out where he was going and how it all fits together. "Yes, it is a challenge," I replied. "But every one of our Entered Apprentices is assigned an instructor and a mentor (two different Brothers). And we have regular Masonic Education programs on Masonic History, Masonic Philosophy, Masonic Symbolism, and even Masonic Philanthropy. We get many of the newly raised Master Masons to prepare a program about their Masonic journey from EA to Master and present it in front of the Brothers. Heck, John, most of the newly raised Brothers and many of the working EA's and FC's are working in some of the parts of our EA and FC degrees. It's just amazing watching all these new and young Brothers soaking up Masonry."

John had stretched his hands out wide as I finished, "Do you see what I am talking about now? Opening your Lodge in an EA Degree is a big part of all you do. A big part of holding on to your newly made Masons, but still not the only part. One of my mentors in business, when I was younger, told me all the time that '*If you want big things to happen, you have to do all the little things,*' and that is what your Lodge is doing, all the little things, and it is why you are so successful.

Brother Chris, all our new Brothers, want Masonry. They don't want to be patted on the back and be told, welcome to the Fraternity. They want to experience the Masonry that they want to LEARN. That is what we promised them, and that is what we need to give them. If they don't get it, they will either stop attending meetings or go away. That is the biggest reason why we lose new EA's. You can open in an EA Lodge all you want, but if you don't have the infrastructure to teach and mentor new Brothers, you might as well open in a Masters Lodge and forget it." Well, I was feeling pretty good by now, "Thanks, John. You made my day. I was pretty confused there for a while."

"That's good," he said as he slid out of the booth and headed towards the door. "Maybe you won't whine and moan about buying my lunch this time."

Well, this is definitely the last time," I called after him more for my pride than anything; I think I heard him laugh as the door closed behind him. I didn't care about getting stuck with the bill again. Usually, when I sit and have Masonic communication with another Brother, I am rewarded by the answer or key to the answer to my question or problem. As I sat there reflecting upon this conversation with John, Sally sat the bill down on the table. I motioned to her and handed her my card so she could close out the ticket. I was deep in thought, sipping my iced tea, thinking about the New Year when she returned, and instead of putting the receipt on the table, she slid into a chair opposite me. I looked up, a little surprised and confused. It was apparent she wanted to say something but looked a little uncomfortable.

I waited, and finally, she looked up and asked in a low voice, "You and that man are Brothers, aren't you?"

"Well, I never thought we looked a bit alike," I laughed out loud.

Sally smiled at that, "I don't mean like you have the same parents. I mean like this," as she held out her hand to show me the ring she was wearing. I glanced down, and there on her middle finger was an old and beautiful Masonic ring. She saw the astonished look on my face, and at once, she was embarrassed. "Please don't tell me that I can't wear this ring," she said, her voice quivering. "It belonged to the sweetest, most wonderful man I have ever known. It was my Grandpa's ring, who I never knew. Then it was worn for 35 years by my Dad. I was his only child and I asked for it when he passed away last year. If I am not allowed to wear it, just don't say anything at all, please."

I sure didn't expect this. Heck, my throat had gotten tight on me, and I could barely speak. "First of all," I said with my voice breaking. "No one can tell you that you can't wear that ring. Second, hearing what you just said makes me proud that you are wearing that ring. I am sorry about my Brother, your Dad, and I know he is proud that you have it. And yes, that man and I are Masonic Brothers."

"I saw your rings, and I wanted to say something earlier," she said with a smile, relaxing a bit. "I didn't know what to say. My Dad was such a wonderful man, and everyone loved him. He was so proud to be one of you....one of the Brothers. I heard him talk about his Brothers all the time. I have wanted to be one of the Brothers for so long, but I know I can't."

I could see her eyes welling up and the hurt in them and knew I needed to say something to make her feel better. I don't exactly know where it came from, but I looked at her and said in the most fatherly voice I could muster, "You know, you don't have to be a man to endeavor to have the character and love of humanity that we strive for as Masons. It is not our perceived secrets that make us Masons. It is the strength of our faith in all things good and how we apply our moral lessons that shape our characters as Masons. I can see that you have within you all those qualities that we look for when choosing to accept a new man into the Fraternity. Therefore, in my opinion, you have every right to wear your Father's ring proudly." I then told her about the ladies of the Eastern Star and that by being the daughter of a Mason, she was qualified to be a member. She was still wiping her eyes when she said she had to get back to work. When I stood up, she gave me a big hug and thanked me for what I had said.

Later, driving back to work, I was pretty proud that I had found the words to make her feel better, and as I sat there patting myself on the back, I couldn't escape the feeling that the words I found were not really my words but those of Sally's Father. That knowledge just made me smile a little bigger. I gave a silent thanks to my departed Brother and wished him well.

The Legendary BarnDoor STEAKHOUSE EST. 1963

THE BARN DOOR AND HOW
IMPORTANT IS IT REALLY?

The other day I was headed back to the shop from the doctor's office when Big John Deacon called to inform me that he was hungry and not in the best of moods. I figured that was a double whammy, but the newsletter was close to being sent out, and I needed whatever he had to offer for the good of Masonry. So I looked around and pulled into the parking lot of the Barn Door, a great steakhouse just off the loop, and after giving John the address (even though we ate there a few months back), I went on in to wait for him. It was about fifteen minutes when he appeared at my table looking a little more serious than usual. I asked him if he was ok.

"I'm hungry; let's eat and chat later."

I thought about picking on him, but it just didn't seem like the right time, so I waved at Chandler, our server, and she came right over. I had already warned her about John, so when he ordered a large Fillet, a Chicken Fried Steak, a Tassos potato with each, and some grilled asparagus, she acted like it was no big deal. I ordered a much smaller steak with the Tassos potato, of course. To come here and not order one is considered a crime. This place is one of the best steakhouses in the whole area. Those twice baked with lots of cheese and jalapenos, Tassos potatoes, are legendary in these parts. There is nothing I have ever tried at the Barn Door that isn't outstanding. I forgot to mention that the green garlic salad dressing is the best.

John did make a little small talk while we waited for our food. When it came, though, he wasted no time getting digging right in. I heard him mumble between bites that he thought he remembered that we had come here together before. I shook my head, "Restaurants, food, and you all seem to blend in together sometimes. I wasn't sure we had been here before." John acted as if he hadn't heard and went back to his food.

Finally, John finished. I was anxious to hear what it was that he was in a bad mood about. Chandler had just filled our glasses and set the check down on the table, which John slid quickly over to me. Some things never change, I thought, as I deposited my card on top of it. "So what the heck has got you all riled up, my Brother?"

"It seems," John said quicker than I expected, "that I am angry way too much. I have heard it from several people, including some of my Brothers."

"Well, John, you sure are angry a lot more lately. Maybe you need to take some anger management classes or something. It might make you feel better."

He gave me the patented John Deacon glare and growled, "I don't need no anger management classes. I need people to stop making me angry."

I was at a loss for words. Not that I didn't want to say something, but the truth is that the words to respond to that statement haven't been invented yet. John's logic was hard to dispute, as convoluted as it was. Instead of responding, I decided to act like I hadn't heard it. "So, what was it that made you upset, John?"

"Where do I start," he asked, shaking his head? "There was that thing that happened last week at Lodge. A Brother who had done a particularly sad job of presenting his part in a degree came over to me after it was over and said kind of offhandedly, 'Well, I didn't get it perfect, but it doesn't matter because the candidate doesn't know it.' And then he turned and walked away.

Well, I am here to tell you that it took both Wardens and our Tiler to keep me off of the Brother. I was sure steamed at that kind of attitude, Brother Chris."

"But John," I said with a look of concern that I had to force before I broke out laughing at the mental picture of what John had described. "It sounds like you were going to violate an obligation for sure."

"*Naaaaw,*" he growled. "I was going to keep a smile on my face the whole time."

I couldn't hold it in any longer and started laughing. John didn't laugh with me but instead got an indignant look on his face, "I know it is true that the candidate being initiated has no idea of the many mistakes the Brother may make during a degree. But for the rest of his Masonic career, he knows that his degree was poorly done every time he sees the same degree performed. He didn't receive the best his Brothers could have given him. I know there are few perfect degrees, but there is a big difference between a few minor mistakes made due to nervousness and a Brother or Brothers who don't care enough to get it right."

"Yup, my Brother, I am on your side on that one. I wouldn't be happy with that either. Is that all? That's not a whole lot to be angry with."

"Oh heck no," he said quickly. "I am just barely getting started. I am also always a little irritated by all the Brothers who are only along for the ride. No effort put in and always wondering why they aren't getting anything out. The men I am talking about weren't made Freemasons to become better men or help their Brothers and humankind; they did it because they thought they would get what Masonry promises quickly, and they were going to get it free. It had nothing to do with learning how to be a better man, but rather to show everyone that they were better than everyone else."

"Wow, John," I replied, starting to get into what he was saying. "I do know a couple of those guys."

"I know I shouldn't say this, Brother Chris, but I am going to anyway. If being a Mason is all about you...then you ain't no Mason at all as far as I am concerned."

"But John," I interjected. "What about all those Brothers who are just happy being there. They have no agenda except to just be and enjoy."

"*Are you crazy!*" John exclaimed, looking at me kinda weird. "Masonry has something for almost every man. If your mind is clear and your motives pure, your future as a Mason will always be secure. The truth is that within our beautiful and solemn rituals, we all hear the same words, we all travel the same path, and we all receive the same set of tools. But more and more Brothers never seem to even open that toolbox, never come to any realization, gain any understanding or even the slightest illumination of what was given to them. Have you ever heard the term *ignorance is bliss*? I am not trying to say that our Brothers are ignorant in general, but most are unaware of our Fraternity's deeper beauties and mysteries. Most are satisfied staying in the wading pool of the Craft and never attempt to enter the deep end of the pool. The deep end (to continue the analogy further) takes more work, skill, and knowledge to stay afloat.

All want that knowledge. Even the waders crave that knowledge. But something keeps them from it. I guess for some, it is fear that keeps them at the water's edge. There is no doubt that those who jump into the deep end and actively seek all there is to find are rewarded many times over for their efforts. But those who wade with pure hearts can be as good and happy Masons as any. "

"Well, you have covered a lot of territory Brother John. You said you were just getting started on your anger issues."

John got a sad look and looked down and said softly, "Nawwww, it's just that I am also mad at myself."

Boy, that took me by surprise. "I don't understand, John."

"It's my passion for Masonry. It causes me to expect more from my Brothers than I should. It also makes me angry at myself for not being or doing more than I am. It just never seems to be enough. Heck, my wife says I talk too much, and I complain too much. I should be one of the happiest Masons there is, but sometimes I am just plum angry."

I could tell he was hurting. This was not what I expected at all. I had to say something, and I didn't want to patronize him. John said the right words to me many times when I needed them. I still don't know where it came from, but I said, "John, you can never be angry for being passionate. We......you, and I, and hundreds of thousands of Brother Masons are doing something special. Something important. It would help if you remembered that we don't stop, and we don't give up. We can't give up on ourselves, and we sure can't give up on the Craft. There are so much bigger things at stake out there than just us, John."

John looked up, wiped something from one eye, smiled, and said, "Brother Chris, thank you for that. That's just what I needed." We both got up. It was an emotional moment. No words were needed. The feel of that special grip and our love of one another as Brothers and our love for the Craft was all that was needed. I watched the Big Guy walk out the door, hoping that it wasn't the last time I would see him.

WE MAKE ITALIAN BECAUSE WE ARE ITALIAN.

Gabriella's
ITALIAN
GRILL & PIZZERIA

GABRIELLA'S AND SOME MASONIC REFLECTION

You know, I can't say that I would do anything for a free meal, but when John called me and told me he would buy me lunch, I just couldn't say no. Even when he told me I had to meet him some distance south of town. The thought that John was scamming me crossed my mind because he usually finds some way to stick me with the tab anyway. John mentioned that he had a taste for some Italian food. There is a place John had eaten at before called Gabriella's. He liked it, and if I wanted a free lunch, I had better get on my horse and meet him. Well, I haven't named my truck or any of my vehicles like John named his (except for a couple of names I called it when it wouldn't start), so I will say I jumped in my truck and headed south, hoping to get there before all the food was gone.

I arrived just after John did and found him sitting against one wall of the dining room with a gloomy look on his face, staring off into space. I slid into the chair across from him and asked how he was doing. He looked over at me and shook his head slowly, and said in a kinda, sad voice, "I'm ok, Brother. I am just feeling a little melancholy. I just got back from the Valley, and the wind was blowing like the dickens. The dust was terrible, and I have been coughing and hacking for three days. I don't feel good, and I am in a bad mood."

"I am sorry, John. You do look bad and sound terrible. So why did you want to meet for lunch? When I feel bad, I don't want to be around anyone."

"I don't really know," he said slowly with a little smile. "Except that, I didn't want to eat alone. But, I know that the newsletter is getting close to needing to get done, so I figured what the Hell."

John went silent all of a sudden, looking at the menu. I saw him look up across the room a couple of times and figured he was looking for a waiter, so I flagged one down. The waiter quickly got our drink orders and went to get them for us. Soon he was back with two iced teas and said he was ready to take our order. I went first and ordered Lasagna because I like Lasagna and because John had told me it was the best. I was informed that it came with unlimited salad and bread, which was good enough for me.

He then turned to John, who said, "Bring me two of them there, Lasagna Plates with all the fixins. I also want a bowl of that spinach/artichoke dip as an appetizer (which I knew he wasn't going to share) and throw a medium sausage and mushroom pizza in there too." Obviously, they had served John before because the size of his order didn't cause a stir at all. When the waiter asked if there was anything else he wanted, John looked up, "Yes, there is. Every time I look across the room, there is a feller over there staring at me. I don't even know him. Can you ask him not to stare at me?"

The waiter and I looked simultaneously towards the other side of the room, and the only thing in John's line of sight was the opposite wall about 40 feet away. The wall was a mirror which made the whole room look much bigger. I looked at the waiter, he looked at me, and the pained look on his face at the realization that John was probably looking at himself was almost too much to bear. I tried hard not to laugh out loud. In John's defense, the lighting in the room was low, but the waiter and I both could see well enough. I could see the waiter struggling to keep a straight face too. Finally,

I just couldn't let it go, and I asked John which guy he was talking about. He looked over, and sure enough, he was looking at himself in the mirror.

Before I could say anything, John muttered under his breath, "That's him right there." Then he gave a kind of wave which, of course, was simultaneously returned. He then shrugged and looked up at the waiter and said, "Oh heck, he seems like a friendly enough sort. Don't worry about telling him anything, and looked back down." I was holding on by a thread, and I looked at the waiter whose mouth was hanging open as he looked at John with total disbelief. That's when I lost it. I laughed out loud for several minutes, with John looking at me like I was crazy. The waiter walked away, shaking his head. I didn't have the heart to tell John, so I asked him if he had anything for the newsletter to change the subject.

To my shock and surprise, John said, "No, I don't." I must have looked like I had been slapped because he quickly continued, "I am still aggravated about a lot of the same old things, and I am sure your readers don't want to hear the same things over and over."

"I agree, John, but I count on you having something profound to say. Heck, the title of the column is about you."

"*Hey now, Brother Chris,*" he shot back a little defensively. "Don't get yourself too excited. We'll figure something out. Surely there is something that you have going on that we can talk about."

Yes, I was getting overexcited! The column isn't the Profound Pontifications of Brother Chris Williams for crying out loud! Brothers didn't read the article to hear what I had to say. It was all about John.

I opened my mouth to complain, but before I could say anything, our food showed up. I knew there was no talking to John now because he had a pile of food in front of him. He totally ignored me and set about consuming with serious concentration every single scrap of food within arm's reach. Watching him, it was not hard to imagine that leftovers in the Deacon house were pretty much non-existent. As I sat there enjoying my Lasagna, just as John had said, it was the best; I had time to think about John's words. Was there anything going on with me that we could talk about? I thought and thought about it, and the harder I tried, the less I came up with. Most everything at my Lodge and the Fraternity, in general, was good, and I really had nothing much to complain about. This was not good. I didn't know what we would do, but I did know it was John's fault.

Then as I sat there enjoying my lunch, something did pop into my mind. I remembered that Jerod, one of my Lodge Brothers, texted me a couple of weeks before with a picture of a bumper sticker he had seen on a car that he was sitting behind in traffic. When I saw it, I was a little shocked because it was not only blatantly false in its claim but a serious accusation printed on a bumper sticker. I figured that John would surely have an opinion about that. I finished as usual before him as he had about four times more to eat than I did and pulled the picture of the bumper sticker up on my phone to show him. There on the back bumper of a car was a sticker, "*Freemasonry, the Seed of Evil,*" and John Quincy Adams' signature was below it. John took my phone and squinted his eyes to see the picture. I guess I should have told him that he could blow it up so he could see it better but....

John smiled, "Ahhhh, yes, I remember reading about John Quincy. He was our 6th President and got beaten out by Andrew Jackson, who was a Mason. He really never got over the bad feelings of that defeat. Adams was also active and outspoken concerning the events surrounding the Morgan affair. I remember seeing a quote of his that said that no true

Christian could ever be a Mason. Heck, he wrote a whole book on the evils of Masonry."

"But that's pretty bad, John. First of all, it's not true, and secondly, something like that shouldn't be on a bumper sticker. I haven't ever seen a bumper sticker or a sign that says something as bad as that about any organization."

"Actually," John said slowly. "It might be more good than bad."

"*Whaaaaat?!!*" I snapped back at him, probably a little louder than I meant to. "How can you say that? Has that Lasagna overload killed off most of your brain function, and the remaining cells are running for their lives?" I don't have a clue what set him off, but he was just silent for a few seconds, and then I saw a slight smile start to form. That smile became a grin and the grin a chuckle, and then he leaned back and let loose with a long rolling laugh that had everyone in the room looking our way. Most of the diners laughed too, even though they didn't know why. I knew then he had lost his mind, and I had sent him over the edge.

Just as I was about to dial 911, he grabbed his napkin and wiped the tears out of his eyes, "I was imagining those brain cells running for their lives from a piece of Lasagna. Seriously, Brother Chris, you have to understand that there have always been, and there will always be, those who dislike and hate us and our Fraternity. But you have to try to understand why they hate us. To us, it seems ridiculous because *we are Masons*, and *we know what we are*. Those that hate us don't *know* who we are. You and I have beaten to death all the reasons why our Fraternity is hated so much by certain people. I don't think I have ever seen a company or organization of any kind that has all the negative things written about it that Masonry does. We know that we bring some of it on ourselves because too many of our

Brethren do not know how to verbalize what Masonry is or what Masons do. But we haven't talked much about the effect the negative articles on the internet or the books denouncing the Craft as evil or anti-religious have on our Fraternity.

Now I don't claim to be the smartest Brother around, and I could be totally off base about this, but I think that all the negative things actually may help us. I think it's safe to say that all the negativity doesn't hurt us all that much. The Morgan affair did hurt the Fraternity with respect to membership, and you can say that it was devastating to a certain extent. Still, I might argue that most of those Brothers who gave up their Masonic membership over the Morgan affair might not have had the character to be true Masons in the first place. There is no doubt that those who turned their backs on the Fraternity permanently and never returned probably never had Masonry in their hearts. Who knows, possibly that purge might have done more good for the Fraternity than bad in the long run. Masonry has stood the test of time. If there existed within the Craft the evil that extremists contend, it would have been exposed to the world long ago. Men of low character have infiltrated our Lodges from time to time. Their only purpose is to satisfy their misguided and uninformed belief that Masonry has some deep dark ulterior motive other than simply making good men better. And when they find out that there is no conspiracy, no evil, of course, they remove themselves from the organization. But that doesn't satisfy their need to disrupt and destroy. Just like we take the symbols of Masonry to help teach our moral lessons, they take some of those same symbols and attempt to convince others that their meanings are evil. These sad people have hate in their hearts and will spread that hate in any way they can. Fortunately for us, we are not the only thing they hate. Unfortunately for them, their accusations cannot be sustained because they are easily proved false. And so Masonry survives and will continue to survive."

"Ok, John," I interrupted, even though I know that irritates him. "I understand all of that. But how does the negative stuff help us? It doesn't make any sense to me."

John gave me a withering stare, which I expected, before giving me his testy reply, "My Brother, Masonry first and foremost is about quality, not quantity. However, the more Masons we make, the more influence for good we can have on our world. The answer to every problem our Fraternity has, whether real or imagined, is our failure to practice true Masonry. True Masonry is light, and light is knowledge. Therefore Masonry is knowledge, purely and simply, knowledge. Masonry must be *Learned, Practiced, and Passed*. It is that simple. Everything else we do, from our dinners and fellowship to our family programs, to our charitable activities, and everything else, is just icing on the cake. But too much of the time, we consume only the icing and leave the cake."

Then he stopped and looked around and waved our waiter over and asked, "What kinds of cake do ya'll have?"

Well, I thought my mind was going to explode. I almost reached across the table and grabbed him, "*Wait, wait, wait, you can't just stop in the middle of that talk and ask for cake.*" John ignored me, as usual, and asked for a double slice of double chocolate....or in his words, "choke-let" cake. The waiter left to get John's cake, and he turned back to me and said, "Ok, now where was I?"

"You were about to get happily beaten by your Brother," I said through clenched teeth. "I understand the cake and icing analogy completely. And I know that our membership issues have everything to do with most Lodges' failure to give our Brothers, both new and old, what they thought they would get when they submitted their petition. And I know that it stems from the fact that Masons can't just practice Masonry and teach this system of moral development as it was meant to be taught, without injecting their ideas of what men want and what they don't. What I want to know is how anti-Mason statements and writings help rather than hurt us. And no cake until you finish." I knew I had about as much chance of enforcing that last statement as I have of winning the Lotto, but I was hoping to get him to concentrate.

"Ok, Brother Chris," John said with a half-smile. "I believe, and this is my opinion only, that most men who see something like that bumper sticker don't even care about it and will never give it a second thought. There will be some who will cluelessly agree. But there will also be some who will see that and wonder what it all means. Those will be men and maybe some women who are inquisitive, intelligent, and thinking people who will want to know what the heck it all means and will take a moment to find out. When they do, and they see that Masonry is a good and worthwhile organization, I believe that the seed of them becoming Masons is planted. As for a woman seeing it, I think that any woman would be happy to have her husband be part of an honorable organization such as Masonry. So her learning the truth about our Fraternity can only be a good thing. These are the kind of men that we need in Masonry, and as for the bad bumper sticker, there is nothing to fear from anti-Masons because of our order's pure and honorable principles. They have tried to destroy Masonry many times and have consistently failed because Masonry is good. You cannot destroy good."

Just then, John's cake arrived, and I was left alone with my thoughts. It takes John a while to get to the point sometimes, as it is with many Masons, I know, but I usually like it and agree with it when he does. I hoped I could write it all down without losing the importance of some of his words. I sure do wish that all Lodges and Masons would get back to being students and teachers. I liked *Learn, Practice, and Pass.* Learn how to be a Mason. Practice the teachings and lessons in all your daily life. Then, pass them on to your Brethren and all of humankind.

My daydreaming was interrupted by John's agitated voice. He had finished his cake and was looking across the room again. "Dang, if that old boy ain't still a looking at me, I am just going to have to go over there and see what it is he is staring at."

"Whoa up there, John," I said quickly. Maybe you ought to just forget about it. He hasn't caused you any trouble."

"You are right, Brother Chris, but he just won't stop. I ain't caught him looking anyplace else, and it's starting to bother me."

"But John, going over there is not going to make you feel any better," I said softly. "Trust me on this. Consider this one Brother whispering good counsel in another Brother's ear."

He was staring at the wall, and then without another word, John abruptly stood up and made a beeline for the wall. Of course, what he saw was the "other guy" quickly getting up and walking towards him, which startled him a bit because he suddenly stopped, a little unsure all of a sudden. It was pretty comical. John and the "other guy" are standing there staring at each other. It looked like the beginning of an old episode of Gunsmoke and the gunfight each episode started with. Suddenly John took one step, as did his reflection, and then another and then one more, and he stopped. By this time, John's weird behavior got the attention of all the diners and employees in that part of the room. They were sitting there enthralled by John having a showdown with his reflection in the mirror on the wall. I was like everyone else, frozen in place, waiting to see what was going to happen.

Suddenly I saw his body language change as he realized his mistake, and like a slap in the face, it hit me that he was going to be embarrassed in front of everyone. Honestly, I don't care if he gets embarrassed in front of me, but I didn't want him to be embarrassed in front of the whole room full of people. I don't even remember getting up, but I quickly walked past him, pointing at the floor next to the mirror wall motioning him to follow. John complied with a confused look on his face. Finally, we got to the wall, and I bent down and placed my ring that I had taken off on the floor so that no one could see. Then I picked it up and handed it to John. He looked at it for a second, and then the realization hit him, and he smiled, grabbed my hand, palmed my ring back to me, gave me a big John Deacon hug, and whispered in my ear, "I should have listened to the good council." Then John turned and walked out the door. I walked back to the table to get my coat, and all I could do was laugh. There on the table was our bill. Some things never change.

Y'all get back to being students and teachers, ok? There's a lot of happiness in it.

Masonic Philosophy 101 And The Breakfast Tacos Of Champions

The noise was so loud it felt like my head was going to explode. I couldn't figure out where it was coming from, then suddenly something hit me in the back, hard that's when I woke up from a sound sleep. The phone was ringing. The blow to the middle of my back came from Pam, followed by an order to "*Answer the Phone*!!!" There wasn't enough time to focus and read the caller ID, so when my hand finally found the handset, I just pressed the button. That was my first mistake of the day. The second was that I didn't just hang it up right then. I still wasn't awake all the way when I heard the familiar voice of Big John Deacon.

He was talking way too loud and way too fast, "Helloooo, Brother Chris, I thought I would catch you on your way to work and see if we could have breakfast." By the time he finished the first sentence, my mind had cleared; I had glanced at the clock.

"What the heck are you calling me at......." I looked again at the clock. "*Oh my God, John, it's 4:30 in the morning,*" I yelled into the phone, causing another blow to my back from Pam. "*Are you crazy? It's too early even to have breakfast.*"

"Awwww, quit whining, Brother. I need some direction. I am hungry, and I need to know where to go."

By this time, having been rudely awakened, sarcasm and anger were starting to kick in, and I flatly said, "I'll tell you where you can go." Before I could relay that particular destination to him, one more blow landed on my back with the warning, "Be nice!" Grrrr, in my then condition being nice was not my first choice. I realized that I would not win this with the enemy on both sides, so I took a deep breath and told John to meet me at Bill Millers in 30 minutes. I heard him whining about not wanting BBQ for breakfast as I hung up. He would find out in a few minutes that Bill Miller has pretty darn good breakfast tacos. I know because I have one almost every morning.

I hurried through my shower. When I got to the restaurant, John was already inside. They had just opened up and were heating the food up as John stood there looking at the menu, smacking his lips. As I walked up next to him, I smiled at Sarah, who knows me as a potato, egg, and cheese taco with an unsweetened iced tea refill cause that's what I get every day. She already had my taco and tea ready and then nodded to John. She had a questioning expression on her face. I told her that he was becoming one with the menu.

"He has been staring at the menu for several minutes," she said. "I thought he had fallen asleep."

"Nope, he's not asleep," I answered. "He is just coming up with a plan."

Without taking his eyes off the menu, he growled, "You know, I can hear you both. And neither of you are funny." Then, looking down at Sarah, he began to order. "Since my Brother Chris is buying breakfast, I think I will have three of those potato, egg, and cheese tacos. Also, I want three Carne Guisada with cheese tacos. After that, I have to try a couple of sausage and egg tacos and a couple of bacon and egg tacos and add about four bean and cheese tacos for later, and I will be in good shape. And Darlin, I will have some tea also."

"I don't think that good shape is something you ought to worry about, Brother John, unless you consider watermelon a good shape." As he glared at me, I silently calculated in my mind. As best as I could figure, he was getting ready to consume, along with generous portions of sausage, bacon, potatoes, beans, and Carne Guisada, at least a dozen eggs and a dozen tortillas. Heck, that wasn't breakfast; it was a whole week's worth of groceries.

Sarah handed us our drinks and called out the cavalry to get busy making tacos. When they were done, it took two trays to haul it all out to our table, and one for the tacos and one for all the hot sauce and pico de gallo John requested to put on everything. Pico de gallo or peck of the rooster is fresh jalapenos, onions, tomatoes, and cilantro all mixed together. I looked across the table at the mountain of breakfast tacos and heard John oohing and aahing over how good it all tasted. Then, realizing John would be a while, I called Leonard to tell him I would be a little late to work. I was not going to be dragged out of bed this early by John and not get something to put in the newsletter, even if I had to force it out of him.

The morning crowd was filing in to get their tacos, and John's pile attracted a lot of attention. I just kept my head down and avoided eye contact, waiting for him to finish. Soon John was done. I informed him that it was rude to wake someone up as early as he did me without a day's prior warning. He told me that he had a big meeting early this morning and had gotten to town the night before and spent the night waking up hungry. I listened closely but never got anything that remotely resembled an apology, so I shook my head and moved on. "I hope you have something really good for me this month, and you need to start talking because I have to get to work."

"Well, I don't have much, but one thing has been making me think since it happened." I groaned.......the day looked like it was going to get worse. I leaned back and motioned for him to bring it on.

John took a deep breath and began, "On our way out of Lodge after our last Stated Meeting, several Brothers had assembled just inside the front door. Among them were a newly passed Fellowcraft and his instructor. The instructor shared that the new Fellowcraft tried to assign meaning or symbolism to every word and phrase in the degrees and laughingly made everyone think that the Brother was wearing him out with all the questions. However, the new Brother was enjoying the joke, and as I walked up, he turned to me and asked what could be the meaning behind one of the questions asked in the esoteric work of his first degree.

The question concerns how he knew there was a door blocking his path. The answer verifies the fact by reminding him that he could not proceed, and later on, he could. In true amateur shrink form, I asked him what he thought it meant. Due to his short time as a Mason, he could come up with nothing that told him why this particular part of his degree was important. After a few moments of the group waiting for my answer, and none of the others offering an opinion, I told him, 'I believe that, because you were in the dark at the time, that it was to impress upon you that entrance into a Lodge was not something automatic or easy. There were tests to pass, promises to be made, and passwords to be given before you would be trusted with the knowledge and beauty to be found on the other side of that door.' I waited a couple of seconds for a response, but none was offered, just a few nods and a far-off look in the student's eyes.

I left them contemplating my answer, and as I drove home, I got to thinking about the Brother attempting to make sense out of all that had happened to him. I acknowledged sadly that way too many Brothers, new and old, have no desire to attempt to understand or make sense of their lessons. Many others take a literal view of all that was taught to them and, with only a basic understanding of their working tools, are perfectly content with working at just a basic level of Masonry and often reject the deeper philosophical study and discovery.

This rejection is not necessarily because they aren't interested in the deeper meanings. A few years ago, I read a book that explained some of the deeper meanings. There was a phrase that stuck in my mind, and it is why many Masons don't dig into the deeper meanings and mysteries of the Craft. The phrase was, 'Always in new knowledge; we meet new intellectual frustrations because every answer searched for and found, creates new questions."

"Oh wow," I blurted out without realizing it. "That's absolutely true ….and it is frustrating sometimes. But still, it's all good."

"As I said," John snarled at me, obviously irritated that I threw my own opinion in there, "it's not that they aren't interested in the deeper meanings and philosophy, in many cases, they don't have the time to continue searching for more and more answers." I nodded vigorously but didn't interrupt as he rolled on, "This old world has changed so much in just one generation, from a time when people actually had time for reflection, and time to read and study, to a world that is moving so fast, it is all but impossible to keep up. The men and women of this generation are growing their families in a time where their children are involved in sometimes two, three, or more activities outside the school and church. Both husband and wife are being pulled in many, many different directions every minute of every day. We are asking good men, our Brothers, to spend time that most of them don't have, in thoughtful reflection….in the study of their lessons and in search of new meanings and truths within themselves. Then we are disappointed in them because they don't seem to be spending enough of that time.

Well, I assure you that they are more disappointed than we are because they can't. If there ever was a case for a strong Masonic Education program in our Lodges, this is it. I am not sure that this will explain it properly, but Masonry is like a motor in a car. It has many different parts and systems. If the motor is to run, all the parts have to do what they are supposed to, when they are supposed to."

I must have looked like I was not getting what he was saying because he frowned and said with an exasperated voice, "Brother Chris, I used the motor analogy to make sure you understood it. You run an auto shop, for God's sake. It ought to be easy for you."

"You need to climb about two steps down off my rear end, there, Brother," I shot back at him. "I was getting it just fine, just waiting for you to make your point."

John shook his head slightly like I was full of it and continued, "Like I was saying, I see Masonry as an intricate combination of words, symbols, emotions, and timing. All the different parts are equal in importance to the motor running properly, including the timing. When a man petitions a Lodge for the degrees, the motor starts, and as the process works through the reading, investigation, and then to the ballot, the motor gains RPMs. You understand RPM's, don't you?" John said with a sarcastic grin.

As I fought the urge to reach across the table and beat him vigorously about his head and shoulders, he continued, "As the candidate is initiated into the Lodge, and with the motor RPMs getting higher, he learns his work and becomes a Fellowcraft. He learns that work and finally is raised to the sublime degree of a Master Mason, and then learns his Master's work. Our new Brother has now learned all the fundamentals and is now ready to begin his journey of self-improvement and self-discovery. That motor is cruising now and running perfectly, just the way it was intended. But, right about now is where things start breaking down. That valuable part of that motor called time malfunctions. More often than not, the new Master Mason comes to the distressing realization that he is on his own from this point forward. He probably was never given an experienced Brother to be his mentor. His instructor, who may have mentored him to a certain extent, has other students to teach or may only have the questions and answers to give and not the meanings and now seems not to have any time for him. He attends meetings in hopes of finding that light he was told would be available to him.

Instead, he has to listen to the usual motions and reports and a word-by-word reading of the minutes of the last meeting, which he sees as redundant since he was at that previous meeting and heard all of it then. He understands that business is part of the meeting but continues to hope for more knowledge of the Craft. He sits through other degrees hoping for things to become clearer, all the while wishing he had the time to read and study, knowing that with his obligations to his job and his family that attending Lodge meetings is all his schedule will allow. While he enjoys the fellowship of his Brethren, the reasons why he became a Mason, the promise of more profound moral and spiritual truths, and finding an understanding of his inner self does not seem to be a possibility. The RPMs of his motor have dropped significantly, and soon, feeling unfulfilled and maybe a bit taken advantage of, he allows himself to be drawn into other things and stops coming to Lodge. He may continue to pay his dues out of a feeling of duty or obligation to something once believed in, but his growth as a Mason ultimately stopped as soon as he was raised.

What all of our Brethren need to understand is that timing is very, very important. A Brother's journey must proceed immediately after his being made a Master Mason. The lack of Masonic education being given in the Lodges and especially at stated meetings effectively stops a Brother from growing within our Craft system and renders all of Masonry ignorant of its true mission and purpose. Men do not become better men just because of the three degrees. The degrees teach the fundamentals, introduce them to the tools of their new trade, and provide a few basic examples of how to use them. They offer a basic education for a lifetime course of study and discovery. Denying Brothers the higher education we promised them is to make Masonry nothing more than a social supper club with a rather dramatic and interesting entrance requirement. Freemasonry should be a rite of passage and transformation leading to a lifelong journey of building his inner being for the service of God, Family, Self, and all of humankind. This is why so many believe that Masonry has become irrelevant in this day and age.

We say that we do all these great things for men, but we don't. Maybe that is one of the reasons why many of our Brethren are afraid to talk about the Fraternity; perhaps deep down, they see the contradiction between what we are supposed to be doing and what we really do. I see more and more Brothers whose motors have broken down from lack of maintenance and neglect. Disillusioned by discovering what they were promised in Masonry and what they hoped for by being made a Mason, they discover instead a fraternity that had forgotten its purpose, forsaken its duty, and lost its way.

So many Brothers are now wandering in the wilderness, possibly towards that undiscovered country from whose bourn no traveler returns."

John stopped, and I was still writing on my napkin. I had forgotten my recorder and figured I could fill in the middle later if I got the high points. My hand shook as I wrote……. dang, there were all high points, and this was excellent stuff. I looked up at John, and I said, "I know you don't use bad language, Brother John, but I have to say…. Damn, that was good. I didn't know you had that in you."

He had been looking off in the distance, and that word brought him back. He smiled, "I will allow you that one, my Brother because I know how you are." I wondered what the heck he meant by that as he slid out of his chair and announced that he had to get on down the road to his appointment. I was ready to go too. I waved at Sarah, and the crew, who were still in shock from all John had eaten.

I followed John out to his truck and realized that the extra tacos he had ordered for the road he had already eaten. He shrugged and said that he would have to get a snack later. I just laughed and shook my head and told him thanks for the material for the newsletter, shook his giant hand, and watched him roar out of the parking lot in a cloud of dust.

On my way to work, I got to thinking about that new Fellow Craft who was trying to figure it all out, and I hoped that he continued to search for meaning in all that he experienced and that he wouldn't stop at just the most obvious meanings. To do that would be to miss the real reward and beauties waiting for only those who are determined to find the most profound truths and the answers to life's most hidden mystery.

THE GOOD, THE TRUTH AND THE SALT GRASS

My Lodge has what we call a *Philosophic Roundtable* every quarter where we meet at a local restaurant and have dinner and good Masonic fellowship. After dinner, we pose a question or problem about some facet of Masonry and allow every Brother to address his personal views concerning the selected topic. The topic being revealed only just before the discussion makes the discussion more spontaneous and elicits some fascinating and varied responses. Bottom line, it's a heck of a lot of fun as well as engaging Masonic education.

Anyway, 16 of my Brothers and I were sitting down for dinner at the local SaltGrass Steakhouse when my phone went off. It was John Deacon calling, and I figured he would tell me he would be in town for lunch the next day. I answered, "Hello, this is the overeating hotline…would you like to talk to a counselor?" I waited, and there was only silence, and then the line went dead. I broke out laughing, and everyone standing next to me wanted to know what the heck was going on? I started to tell them when the phone rang again. Seeing it was John again, I answered the same way, and again the line went dead. Every Brother within earshot heard what I said, and they all wanted to know who I was on the other end. I told them it was Big John Deacon just as it rang again.

As soon as I answered, before I could say anything, John growled, "You can't fool me a third time cause I looked at the number before I dialed it this time. Now, if you will tell me where you are so I can meet you this evening, I will spare you any more of my wrath."

"Hey John," I said, a little surprised. "I didn't know you were in town. You should have called me earlier." I told him where I was, and he was adamant about coming to the discussion and having dinner.... especially when I told him we were at the SaltGrass Steakhouse. I hung up and apologized to everyone that John was going to be joining us. They all seemed glad that he was coming because a few hadn't met him yet.

It sure didn't take him long to get there. I introduced John around and put him at the end of the table to have a little more room. He promptly waved at our waiter and ordered range rattlers, a rack of BBQ ribs, and the large chicken fried steak with extra gravy and garlic mashed potatoes. Most of the guys at the table couldn't hear what he ordered, but when the food came, there was shock on their faces as they saw what John was going to eat for dinner. John had been carrying on a conversation with several Brothers at his end of the table, but as soon as he got his food, he lapsed into total silence while he ate.

The food was darn good, and the conversation between everyone had slowed to almost nothing. We got through dinner without incident, which was surprising. I got up to lay out the topic and question for the discussion and laid out the rules. Now, one of the rules is that what is said inside that room in the discussion is not to leave the room. Not that there are any earth-shattering comments made usually, but it is so that every Brother will feel comfortable sharing whatever point of view he has on the subject. So, keeping that in mind, I am going to allude vaguely to what transpired.

First, the topic/question had to do with explaining your thoughts on a certain part of the Master's degree. I realized early on that it was a pretty deep subject as a couple of Brothers bypassed their turn to collect their thoughts a bit. The comments were as different and as varied as you could imagine. We had 17 Brothers and just as many opinions as it seemed, and several strayed from the original topic and went off in a different direction. When it was John's turn, I told him that he didn't have to participate since it was his first time.

He shook his head, "I would like to say a few things, but I am going to stray off the subject a little." In all the time I had spent with John, I had come to know that he was both a literal and a philosophical thinker, but I really didn't know what to expect from him in this situation. When he said he wanted to say a "few" things, I got a little uneasy because I had told everyone that they had three minutes to say what they wanted to say. I knew how long-winded he could sometimes be. The last thing I wanted was to have him talk for thirty minutes. I looked around, and everyone seemed agreeable, so I nodded to John to go on. He was the last one, and several of the Brothers had not used their full time, so I figured it would be okay.

Instead of standing, John just leaned forward in his chair, "Brethren, Brother Chris and I have been meeting every month for quite a few years now. We have some good old Masonic discussion that he writes down and then puts in that newsletter of y'alls and calls it Profound Pontifications. I don't know how profound it all is, but I was passing through this afternoon and wanted to talk about the article, and when I found out y'all were having this philo.... .phila....philashificle ...ahhhh.... this...... discussion... I wanted to be a part of it....and I was hungry too.

What I came to talk to Brother Chris about is something pretty serious, and it is something we should all be concerned about. How many of you read the Pontifications column in the newsletter?" Most of the hands went up. John nodded and took a deep breath and looked at every Brother at the table with a look of sadness in his eyes, "My Brothers, I know it seems like I whine and moan about stuff all the time, but I do it to point out things that in my opinion are wrong. I had one of my Lodge Brothers come up to me and tell me that I was a complainer the other day. I gotta tell you, Brothers, that it was like a slap in the face. I never thought of myself as a complainer. I felt that I was pointing out things that we could get better at as a Fraternity.

What I want to talk about today is not good, again; I am sorry. But, when I get done, you might think that this is the absolute worst I have ever done for your newsletter and all the Brothers who read the column.......and (looking at me) I will understand if you throw it out. I want you all to know and understand that everything I am going to say, I say out of love for this Fraternity, love for my Brethren, and my passionate belief that this wonderful Fraternity CAN realize its true purpose. We can overcome the evil in this world by changing it one person at a time."

John paused before continuing, "Brothers, what I think stands between our Fraternity as it is and our Fraternity as it should be can be summed up in two short words. These two words represent the most basic principles of this Fraternity and, in my opinion, have been thrown by the wayside, trampled on like some insignificant and unnecessary afterthought never intended to be any more than words that feel good and sound good. Those words are TRUTH and RIGHT.

All Masons should tell the truth, and all Masons should do what is right or make every effort to. Our Brothers were good men when they were accepted into our Fraternity. We assume that since they were good men to start with and to have the benefit of the lessons of the three degrees, they couldn't possibly violate our laws and regulations. But, in an alarming number of instances, we are finding that just the opposite is true."

John paused to take a long breath, and I thought to myself …. *I have been a Mason for plenty of years, and I have seen a few things done that were not right, and I suppose that most were unintentional.* I knew what John was talking about, and I realized that it was probably the wrong time to say it, but I felt like I had to say something. I looked up and down the table and then blurted out, "But John, I realize it may be a problem, but the majority of our Brothers, I think, are honorable Masons who always strive to do the right thing."

"That may be mostly true, my Brother, but should that be enough? Is it enough that *most* Masons do the right thing, and is it enough that *most* Masons follow the rules and abide by the Laws? And is it enough that *most* Masons set a good example to those around them? I say no! For some strange reason, today's society thinks that being close is okay, almost is good enough, and is mostly all we should expect. I say emphatically, Hell no!!! We should be better than that. We should because it is expected of us and because we swore we would……and….and just because."

I looked around, and I saw most of the Brothers were nodding their agreement. I realized that no one had noticed that John was already over his three-minute limit. I decided not to say anything as he was already rolling on, "I see Brothers all the time, not just pushing the limits of their obligations, not just toeing the line between right or wrong, but disregarding those obligations and the Laws and doing what they want to do instead of what they should do. I see way too many times Brethren trying to make Masonry meet their desires and attitudes instead of making themselves, as Masons, conform to the principles of the Order. That attitude is a direct reflection of the current state of our society. In every degree, we take an obligation and make a solemn promise to God and ourselves to abide by the rules and regulations under which we are governed.

We do not promise to abide by only the ones we agree with or only those we want to follow. Heck, I don't agree with every rule or law, but, by God, I promised with my hand on the Holy Book, and so did you, to follow them....no questions asked. Thankfully, I have an avenue to change those laws if I don't think they are right. But until a law is changed, I must follow it. The fact that we even need to talk about this is baffling to me.

Did you know some good men and Masons are internally conflicted between the friendship and acceptance of their Brethren? When they see their Brothers clearly violating Masonic Laws and regulations; it bothers them? Most don't say anything but quietly agonize about it; some go away and continue their Masonic journey at another Lodge or Masonic appendant organization (sound familiar??). Many go away and leave the Fraternity altogether. We have Lodges whose Brothers are bullied into doing things they know are not right but feel that they have no power to push back or are afraid to try. These Brothers need to know that the Lodge is a Democratic form of government and any Mason who bullies, coerces, or even suggests to another Mason to do something that either of them knows is wrong, or against the laws or regulations of our Grand jurisdiction, is committing at the very least a moral offense, if not a Masonic offense, and there are consequences for both. Going along to get along when you know it is wrong is not acceptable. We have lost new Brothers as well as Master Masons from Lodges because they saw things being done without regard to the Laws or principles of Masonry. They were mistreated when trying to do the right thing and felt their only option was to quit."

John was talking faster and louder now, but I knew I couldn't stop him. He was in high gear! "Men come to us sick and tired of being lied to by different institutions and entities in their lives. They have people doing bad things to them and justifying their bad behavior without taking responsibility for their actions. We tell them that Freemasonry teaches a system of Moral behavior where honesty, truth, and integrity are the bedrock principles of our organization? Then they see after going through their degrees that some Brothers don't care what the rules are because that's the way I am going to do it, or that's the way we do it here in our Lodge."

John was temporarily out of breath, and he paused for a few seconds before continuing. Finally, he pointed at the Brother on his right and asked, "What would you say if you found out that there was a Lodge that decided that it was not necessary to teach all the required memory work for each of a Brother's degrees?"

The Brother looked uncomfortable but answered quickly. "I would be shocked that it could ever happen here."

"But if it did," John shot back. "What would you think? What would you do?"

The Brother thought about it for a second and finally said, "I think I would feel betrayed."

John's eyebrows went up in surprise, "Betrayed," he repeated? "I didn't expect that word."

"It was the first word that popped into my head," the Brother said, frowning. "It's like they were stealing from our Fraternity. Stealing away our integrity, stealing away our good name and good deeds."

Another Brother next to me said pleadingly, "Please don't tell me that this is real ……. It's just a hypothetical situation, right?"

John shook his head again sadly, "It is true and what is worse, is that when the new Brother in this situation found out that learning the rest of the work was required and he asked about it, his Brothers those same Brothers who brought him into Masonry got angry and told him that he should have kept his mouth shut."

"No way," I said, not wanting to believe it!! "You've got to be kidding. This cannot be happening in a Masonic Lodge! This is a Clandestine Lodge, right? One of those that are not real Masons and don't follow any laws or rules?"

"I am sorry, but it is all true," he said, even sadder than before. "And you can be sure that this is not the only thing wrong there."

"I hate even to ask, John, but what happened with this new Brother if all of this is true?" John just stared at me for a few seconds and then looked down at the table. I saw his jaw clench as he prepared to talk, and then he looked up and said, "He quit. He handed back his EA card, and he quit. He walked away from Masonry, completely disgusted. He said that he had lived 45 years of his life without being a Mason, and he could live the rest without us too."

The Brothers at the table looked like they were in shock, and one at the other end of the table asked, "Well, what is a Brother supposed to do, John, when he feels he can't change anything that he knows is wrong?"

"Well, there are several options. First, they need to know that they are probably not the only one in their Lodge that sees and knows things are not being done right and who would like to see things changed. They need to find those Brethren (and there will be more than they can believe) and start to build a consensus. And they need to start voting and changing their Lodge, and it can and will happen. It will require some pain, and there will be hard feelings, but in the end, the Lodge will emerge as a good Lodge, with *Just and Upright* Brethren….and good Masons doing things right.

Secondly, and while this is an option, it is not one that I would recommend, but it would need to be made known by a Brother or Brothers who seek to make the proper changes to their Lodge that those who are violating Masonic law will have charges filed against them. Then those who are guilty will either change their ways, they will leave, or they will have charges filed. This is ugly and uncomfortable, but if necessary, the right thing to do is save the Lodge and start doing things right. And thirdly, if the previous options are not feasible, then there are plenty of Lodges out there that ARE following the laws and regulations. They should find one and make a change. I know it's hard to leave your mother Lodge, but you cannot and should not give up on Masonry because of a few un-informed Brothers. You and your journey are worth more than that. We need to remember that we are here to take those principles of the Order and put those working tools to use to become better moral men."

John was lightly pounding his hand on the table as he made his point. "We are here to serve each other, to serve our families and our communities, and to serve humankind. That is the purpose of Masonry. Our Masonic lessons teach us to do right and to do good in all things. There is pride in doing things right, but there is no pride in not doing them right. I recently went on an investigation of a petitioner. As I usually do when he answers why he wants to be a Mason by simply saying that he wants to be a better man, I refuse to accept that as an answer. I ask him again and get a similar answer. The third time I ask, I want to know where the first idea came from to become a Mason and why. This particular man blew me away because he looked down for a couple of seconds, and when he spoke, he said that he was sick and tired of being lied to by everyone….the media, the government, even his friends. He was sick and tired of people doing stuff wrong and then not taking responsibility for their actions. He heard about the Masons and, because of what he had read and researched, wanted to become a Brother to be around men who told the truth and did things right.

That, my Brothers, is what Masonry should be, that man's ideal picture. But, what happens when he becomes a Mason only to find out that all Masons don't do the right thing or tell the truth? What then?"

We all looked at each other, trying to decide who would answer, only to realize that he was rhetorical because John continued right on. "Doing right should extend to everything we do as Masons. We should expect excellence in all things Masonic and in our private lives as well. Excellence in the ritual, including opening and closing the Lodge, and in all degree work. Do we demand perfection? *No! But excellence, yes!!* When a Brother enters his Lodge, it should be a special place where he knows that the burdens of life can be put aside for a time and that he knows that what is done in his Lodge is done right. That feeling is what draws him back to the Lodge again and again and to his Brethren. It is a great feeling of pride and accomplishment when a Brother belongs to this kind of Lodge.

When he walks out the Lodge door and steps back into the outside world, because of the lessons he learns and the principles he adheres to within the Lodge he is reenergized to carry on his work as a just and upright Mason and make that difference in his life as well as the lives of others. A lodge that does not practice excellence and adherence in all things Masonic is a Lodge in turmoil and unhappiness. Peace and harmony don't mean just some Brothers in the Lodge....it means all Brothers in the Lodge."

As John sometimes does, he abruptly stopped and leaned back in his chair. The other 15 Brothers at the table and I just sat there staring at John, nodding our heads, waiting for him to continue. When they realized he was done, several applauded, and others told him he was right. They agreed with him. His sashay down a completely different path than the one we started the discussion on made everyone forget what we were talking about in the first place. Interestingly, he had spoken for almost 17 minutes, and no one pointed out he was over the time limit. I got up and thanked everyone for coming, and one by one, all the Brothers shook hands all around and filed into the outer room to pay their checks.

Soon John and I were the only ones left in the empty room. He just sat there and didn't seem to want to leave. I moved down to a chair next to him and asked him if he was okay. He said in a low voice, "I am sorry for the gloom and doom, Brother."

"It was a Hell of a talk, John," I replied, and I added, "Someone had to say it."

John looked at me and smiled without humor, "You don't understand, Brother Chris. We shouldn't have to talk about this. We shouldn't ever have to talk about this." He slowly got up and shook my hand and gave me a John Deacon hug, and said in almost a whisper, "Who is going to show the world what good is and what truth is if not us? Who?" John turned and walked out the door.

We asked the wait staff not to come into the room during our discussion, and they had complied well. But as I sat there alone and contemplating, two of them came in to ask me if they could clean up. I nodded. As they were cleaning, one of them turned to me and told me that the waiters all voted and decided that we were part of the Illuminati. I could only laugh and shake my head no. He turned to the other one and said,

"They are Freemasons, I'll bet, but don't ask them cause they won't tell you."

So, I spent the next 30 minutes telling them what Masonry is and what Masons do. And yes, I had to pay John's tab.

CHILITOS EXPRESS AND THE ....
METAFORMINAS

John Deacon was, at the moment, the farthest thing from my mind. It was a slow Friday, and we were catching up on a bunch of stuff at the shop when my cell phone rang. I looked at the caller ID and saw who it was, and for a split second, I fantasized that John was calling me to buy *ME* lunch. Ok... Ok ...I said it was a fantasy.

I hit the talk button and got an earful of a super happy John who told me that he had found a great place to eat and I needed to come right now. I asked where it was. John gave me the address, and I grabbed my keys and headed that way. I didn't recognize the address, so I put it on my phone's navigation. It was a little concerning when the navigation gave me the directions but noted nothing at that location. I couldn't remember anything I had done to John that he would need to get back at me, so I called him to find out what was going on. John did not answer, so I followed the navigation and figured I would play it out to the end. Boy, what a surprise I got when I pulled up to the address. There sat "his humongousness" at a rickety picnic table that had seen better days, under a big umbrella with enough food to feed a medium-sized Boy Scout Troop scattered all over the table. A few feet from him was a food truck on wheels semi-permanently placed in that spot. On the side of the truck/trailer was a sign that said *Chilitos Express*. I have to tell you that I had some misgivings about even getting out of the truck, but the smell coming from that truck was like an invisible pair of hands pulling me towards the order window. Heck, I have no self-control when it comes to great food, so I allowed those hands to pull me right out of the truck.

I paused on the way at John's table to see what he was consuming. Instead of a greeting, he looked up at me with that wary warning look that my big hound dog gives me when I get close to her food bowl while eating. I know the look well and what it means. I want to say I was amazed, but I can't because I wasn't. Lord, there were the remains of two hamburgers with some onion relish and what looked like cream cheese and jalapeno tamales.... mmm looked good. Also, he was munching on a huge sandwich that looked like it had one of everything you could put in a sandwich. I just shook my head and turned towards the order window. John yelled out over my shoulder to the guy at the window that his buddy was here and to treat him nice.

I was greeted at the window by Al, who was very excited to see me. Al told me about everything on the menu. I wasn't listening because I saw the picture of the cheesesteak sandwich, and I am addicted to cheesesteak sandwiches. Immediately I knew what I wanted. I was also giddy with excitement that John had already eaten. This was going to be a cheap lunch. Yippee!!! I ordered the cheesesteak sandwich. I heard John over my shoulder yell out to get him one too. I looked back at Al, and we both just shook our heads in amazement. Al finished taking the order, and I gave him my card to pay. When he handed it back to me, I nearly fainted. There were way too many numbers before the decimal point. I looked back at Al and said maybe a little too sarcastically, "I am not buying a car here, buddy, just lunch."

"Your friend said he forgot his wallet and that it was your turn to buy lunch anyway," Al replied with a frown.

I just shook my head again, which I seem to do a lot of that around John. Walking over to John's table, he started to clear me a spot to sit. I just stared at him and …. yup…. shook my head again, "I am going just to give this receipt to Pam and have her call you."

"But did you tell her that good infor….."

"I told her that, and she was not impressed," I shot back.

"Well, ok, you tell Miss Pam that Big John is buying lunch next month." Before I could respond, a voice from the truck called out that there were two cheesesteaks ready. John was out of his seat in a flash and grabbed those two sandwiches and brought them back. Instead of just sitting one down in front of me, John stood there trying to decide which one was bigger. I reached up and grabbed the one closest to me, and began to eat. John just shrugged and devoured his in silence with a big grin on his face. He looked a little weird. I have to say that that cheesesteak sandwich was one of the best I have ever had and by the noises John was making he agreed. Finally, we were both done, and John seemed to be full enough to talk. He just sat there with that goofy grin on his face.

"You are way too happy, my Brother," I said. "That must mean you have nothing of a profound nature to share with me."

"Why would you say that," he asked?"

"Well, the best wisdom comes out of your mouth when you are sad or angry."

"That hurts my feelings," John said with a big frown.

"No, it doesn't," I countered. "I know you too well. You are in way too good a mood right now for something like that to hurt your feelings. So why are you so happy?"

He got a bigger grin on his face, "For several reasons. First, contrary to popular belief, I watch and listen closely. I see Brethren changing all the time."

"Hmmm, what do you mean changing?" I asked, puzzled.

"You know," John growled impatiently, waving his hands. "Like a met...meta.... morf...morf......"

I jumped in and bailed him out. "Do you mean metamorphosis?"

"Yes yes, that's it.... METAFORMINAS!!" All I could do was shake my head again as he went on. "I see Brothers having those moments and those realizations when something they long thought meant one thing, and they now realize it means something different or something more. When I run into a Brother, and I find out while talking with him that this has happened, it makes me glad because it means he is living his Masonry, asking questions, and seeking new truths. I like it when I get to watch that happen. Once a Brother has one of those meta...metam.... oh hell, you know what I mean. He gets an answer or an understanding he did not have before, creating more questions to answer. He is now compelled to find new answers, which again leads to new questions and new understandings; from there, the search never ends. Of course, the number of Brothers who look for some of those answers is very small. The majority go about their Masonic way, content in the belief that the allegorical aspect of our rituals is all there is. They get the fact that the degrees are moral lessons intended to make us better men, and they are happy in their basic understanding of those degrees. But whether they think there is something more, something deeper, something beautiful in its spiritual aspect, they aren't inclined or motivated to open that door that leads to their inner self. But .... they are still good Masons. Brother Chris, did you look at the funny papers last Sunday?"

Before I could answer, he rolled on. "In the Peanuts column, Lucy and Linus were standing there looking off in the distance. Lucy said that when she grew up, she would climb to the other side of the hill and there find happiness and fulfillment—implying that the answer to everything was on the other side of that hill. Linus thought about it for a second. Finally, Linus said that maybe there was another kid on the other side of the hill, thinking that the answers and happiness and fulfillment were on this side of the hill. And boy, that sure irritated Lucy. She yelled out to the other side to 'FORGET IT!'

"Yeah yeah, I saw it, but what does that have to do with anything?"

"Wha...wha....," John sputtered. "What does it have to DO with anything??? It has everything to do with everything. I know it was supposed to be funny, but if you look at it closely, it explains pretty well the fact that in all our lives, all the answers we seek, all the truths we want......and all the assurances needed are right in front of us. The answers are not on the other side of the fence or the other side of the hill. The truth is that we need to open our minds and broaden our views and allow the light to come in. Ultimately, we and we alone are responsible for our happiness, our success, our strengths, and our weaknesses. Sure, it's much easier to blame someone else for our failures because it lets us off the hook. I think our Brother Claudy said it best, 'The great object of Masonry is not to tell a man what to think but to teach him how to think for himself.'

Last night, I talked to a new Entered Apprentice who told me that he could learn the work faster if it was written down instead of passing it mouth to ear. I asked him why he thought we didn't write it down? He said that it probably was to preserve the secrets, and I answered him by asking, what if I told you that it wasn't necessarily to protect the secrets; what would you say then? He had to think about it for a minute, and then he smiled and said that maybe it had something to do with bonding with one another. That made me smile because he had just realized one of the central tenets of our order, friendship, and Brotherly Love. Then he expressed how he thought it was meaningful that basically, a stranger would voluntarily commit many hours of his time to help him learn his work. I am very optimistic about this Brothers' Masonic journey. It's these kinds of things that make me happy and make me smile. And talking about that mortamefisis thing...."

"It's metamorphosis, John," I cut in.

"Whatever," John growled, momentarily dampening his cheery mood. "I was talking to two of my closest friends and Brothers last week about Masonic philosophy. I could indeed talk to these two Brothers for hours at a time if I could. We have been talking about Masonry, our Masonic experiences, personal views, and our understanding of Masonry for several years. We each know where the other's mind is Masonically. Over the years, I have seen both these Brother's views and opinions within certain parts of our Fraternity change either slightly or more than slightly. I am sure that they have seen the same things in me as well. To some, seeing Brothers changing the way they see and understand some things about the Craft can be disturbing. Still, in reality, change and intellectual, moral, and spiritual awakening are what our teachings are all about. The joy of feeling my awareness increase, and my understanding becomes deeper is, at times, indescribable. This must surely be some of what is called the beauties of Freemasonry."

"It is surely some of the beauties," I said. Now I know why you are so jovial this month."

"But there is more," John said excitedly. "Do you remember the EA that was mistreated in his Lodge that he quit and walked away in disgust?" Apparently, John didn't want an answer because he never paused. "Well, I just got a call from him saying he wanted to continue his Masonic journey, and he wants to do it at my Lodge. He had talked to several other Masons who made him want to continue his work."

"That's pretty cool, John," I replied. "I know how disappointed you were in that whole deal."

"Yes, I was, but that is another one of the beauties of Masonry. Great things happen because of the example of good Brothers. So, yup, it's been a really good week."

As he walked away, I heard him humming the song *Everything's Coming Up Roses* under his breath. John is such a nut sometimes. It was a happy day for a happy guy.

VITEK'S
· Since 1915 ·
WACO, TEX
MARKET

VITEKS, THE SERPENT, AND A LESSON IN MASONIC SECRECY

Those of you who have been regular readers know that I do not believe in luck or coincidence. I now know that things happen how they are supposed to happen. And that knowledge has been such a great awakening because of all I have realized and experienced. What I don't understand is how my Big Brother John Deacon seems to know where I am every month. It's almost like he has some kind of a tracking device on my truck or something...... hummmmm. I might check that out......

Well, anyway, what happened is that I was recently in Waco getting ready to have lunch with two of my closest Masonic Brothers when my phone rings. I saw it was John and figured he would tell me when he was coming through San Antonio so we could meet. The newsletter deadline was coming up fast. I answered, and he said that he was on his way to town and wanted to know if I could meet him the next day for lunch. I told him that I would not be back for three days and where I was in Waco.

"Hey, that's great. I am just passing through Waco now.... I will be right there."

I just stood there with the phone to my ear, no one on the other end cause John had already hung up, a dumb look on my face, and Brad and Larry looking at me wondering what the heck was going on. I told them that there was going to be one more joining us for lunch. They were a lot happier about it than I was; heck, they weren't going to have to pay for him.

We were at Vitek's BBQ just getting ready to get in line to order. I explained to the order taker that we had one more coming and that he was a huge guy who eats like three men. I just wanted to warn him, but right in the middle of my explanation, John walked up and danged if every employee in the place didn't walk up and say hi to him; by name. Apparently, John has been there many times before.

John said hi to all three of us and said, "I'll get us a table." He then walked off. I called out to John that he had to order at the counter first, and he just laughed and kept walking. Then, the guy taking the orders laughed, "Don't worry, we have his order already." We were all confused, but we went ahead and ordered, picked up our food at the end of the counter, and went to look for John.

We found John sitting at a big booth in the back. As surprised as we were that he did not have to order his lunch, he didn't even have to pick it up either. The staff brought it to him. I asked John what he got as he tried to look over the top of the mountain of food in front of him. He said he got his usual which was four full Gut Pacs. A Gut Pac is a big cardboard bowl with a layer of Fritos on the bottom with chopped beef, beans, sausage, cheese, onions, bread, pickles, jalapeno peppers, and BBQ sauce piled on top. Just one was a huge amount of food, and John had four of them. Larry, Brad, and I just had BBQ plates and were finished long before John was.

We made small talk amongst ourselves because John always eats in total silence. Just when we thought he was done, one of the staff came over to shovel .... er...pick up all the trash he left behind. The server left John a big bowl of banana pudding; the whole top was covered in vanilla wafers, just the way I like it. We all looked at that and immediately asked the guy to bring three more and boy, was it good!!! Finally, all the food on the table was gone. I asked John if he had anything worth putting in the newsletter to share with us. He contemplated for a moment, trying to build suspense until I got up and said, "OK, we're outta here… let's go."

"OK, OK," he said, motioning us to sit back down. "I do have a great story for you."

"We'll be the judge of that," I said, smiling at Larry and Brad, who agreed with me.

John blinked a couple of times like he was confused but continued, "We talk about Masonic secrecy, and for most non-Masons, the *secrecy* is Masonry. They don't seem to care about anything else. It's all about the secrecy. Well, last week, I experienced Masonic secrecy in its purest and most perfect form. I had been invited to install my Nephew as Worshipful Master of Chambers Creek Lodge, one of our many historic moonlight Lodges. Coincidentally, as it turned out, I planned to mention Masonic secrecy in my remarks to the non-Masons in attendance. But little did I know that I was going to see Masonic secrecy in action."

John had our full and undivided attention now, and we were all leaning a little forward in our seats. John talks a little loud at times, and I was sure that the guys at the table next to us must have heard him cause they were leaning a little towards us and not talking to each other at all. I gave John the *lower voice* signal, which he totally ignored, so I kept myself ready to jump on him if he said anything he wasn't supposed to.

"Now I am going to tell the story as close to how Brother Joe told it," John started with a serious voice. "This is an ancient Lodge building, over 100 years old, but still standing strong. Originally it was a school on the ground floor and the Lodge room on the top floor, and as you can imagine, pest and varmint control is always a challenge. Brother Joe, the incoming Junior Warden, got to the Lodge before the rest of us and opened up the fellowship hall on the ground floor. He then was going to climb the stairs to the Lodge room and get the lights on. To get to the stairs, you have to exit the lower level and enter a hallway on the side of the building. As he got to the top of the stairs, he saw something move, and when Joe saw what it was, he froze."

At this point, dear Reader, I have to tell you that when John paused to take a swallow of his tea, with me, Larry, and Brad hanging on that last word, he came really close to being roughed up by all three of us....and I think we could have taken him.

John saw the aggravation on our faces and chuckled before finally continuing, "There, against the wall and wrapped around the top of the staircase banister was a snake. They just stared at each other for a few seconds waiting for the other to make a move. Brother Joe looked him over and saw that he was a rat snake about four feet long, and although he knew he wasn't poisonous, that didn't mean he liked him any better. Then symbolically proteming as Tiler, Brother Joe grabbed the implement of that office and used the business end to coax that slithering intruder down the stairs. I can almost see him in my mind thrusting and parrying, keeping that sucker moving downstairs towards the door. Every few feet, that old snake would raise his head and swivel it around to look at Joe as if to say, *give me a break.... I'm going already.* And when that snake got to the door, he went in behind the door instead of just going out. So Joe, really careful like, used the tip of his sword to gently swing the door away from the wall, keeping a watch out for him to try and double back. Instead of the door just swinging away from the wall, it shut completely, and there Joe was.... him and that Rat Snake together......alone....in total darkness.

Now I don't know about you boys, but I would have been up on my tippy toes doing a little tap dance worrying about keeping my bodily functions in check in that situation. But Brother Joe is a braver man than I, and he reached across and opened that door and looked down just in time to see the last 12 inches of serpent disappear through a sizable crack between the door frame and the floor. Then, knowing there were visitors and more than likely ladies coming, he found a piece of wood and covered the escape hatch to prevent any re-entry at least from that spot."

John stopped to take a breath, and I could hear the guys at the next table giggling. Brad's mouth was open in shock, and Larry was shaking his head in disbelief. I just sat there in silence, staring at him. I still wasn't sure that he was not making the whole thing up. "So where does the Masonic secrecy come into play?" I asked.

"Well, if you would hold your horses and let me finish," John shot back sarcastically.

"When the rest of us got to the Lodge, Brother Joe was sitting at one of the tables, still a little winded, holding that Tiler's sword in his hand. After he told us the story, we all went searching the various apartments of the building, upstairs and down, for that unwanted visitor. We then held a quick clandestine meeting to swear everyone to secrecy so as not to have the visitors and ladies refuse to come into the building and cancel the Installation. It was decided that all hands were to keep an eye out to guard against the approach of any kind of cowan or eavesdropper."

"Why was the meeting clandestine?" Brad wanted to know.

"Because we didn't have enough to open a Lodge," John snarled like we already knew that. "And we didn't want anyone to get wind of what happened.......and nothing did. That snake never made an appearance, and all went well."

"So what about your comments before the installation?" Larry asked. "You said you were going to say something about secrecy. How did that go?"

"Well, let me tell you fellers what I told them. I told them that there are a lot of people out there who think our Fraternity is a secret society and that everything we do is secret. I mentioned that it is true that secrecy is at the heart of our lessons, obligations and that our rituals contain supposed Masonic secrets. But as most Brother Masons know, our secret ritual can differ quite a bit from one Lodge to another and sometimes from one night to another in the same Lodge. Also, the ritual from one Grand Jurisdiction to another is either slightly or, in most cases, very different from each other. I told them that the true secrets of the Freemasons are just this: shared experiences, private thoughts, and deeper understandings between men, who have formed a bond through a fraternity that supports and strengthens them through its teachings. Men from all walks of life and all backgrounds come together in Masonry. They call each other Brother. Many of us truly become like brothers. We form trusting and resilient friendships. We share life's trials and tribulations. We accept and are accepted."

"Wow, John. That's really good. How did they like it?"

"Well, if you would quit interrupting like you always do and let me finish, I will tell you," John growled.

"I told them that there are those who believe that Masons are a group of elitists, who parade around in their Aprons, and think they are better than everyone else, but the truth is that Masons are just regular men, good men, who are each on his journey of self-discovery and self-improvement. Masons are men who believe in God and are looking for, and in most cases, they find truths about not only themselves but also life in general.

I told them that we use what we call working tools which relate symbolically to the tools of the ancient builders. In our rituals, these tools are used symbolically to convey moral and spiritual lessons by using allegory or simply a play in which the initiate represents the principal character. I finished by telling them that Masonry speaks to every man differently. It speaks to him in a way he can understand. It is said that Masonry, from the outside looking in, is impossible to comprehend, and from the inside looking out, is impossible to explain. In many ways, it cannot be explained. It must be experienced; it must be felt. It is about doing things right, and it is about good.

If you are a family member of a Mason, you need to understand that Masonry is not to be made more important than your God, family, or vocation. Masons are not perfect men, but we are working on it. The stated purpose of Masonry is to make good men, better men, better husbands, better fathers, and better citizens. To be a positive example and influence to others."

John stopped, and no one said anything. Partly because he chewed my rear last time, anyone said anything, and partly because no words were necessary. There was no doubt it was good…. maybe real good.

The guys at the next table who were eavesdropping got up and came over and shook John's hand and said, "Thank you, sir. That was very interesting. I learned more about you, Masons, in that last thirty minutes than I have ever known. We are glad we were here to eavesdrop. I have family members who are Masons, but I never asked to join because everyone who tried to explain it to me had a different story, and I took that to be suspicious. I am starting to see why it is so confusing to those of us who aren't Masons. I can see that it is different for each man, and that makes sense to me." With that, he and his friend said goodbye and walked out the door.

"That was a pretty good story John," Larry said. "I am not sure that it lives up to the definition of pure and true Masonic secrecy, but it sure puts into perspective our obsession with the word *secrecy*."

"Did you ever stop to think about how long that snake has been hanging around the Lodge? He might already be in possession of all the secrets of a Master Mason. If that is true, my Brother," Brad interjected.

"Maybe y'all ran him off, and he was looking to get a petition. That's a hell of a way to treat a prospective candidate."

We all, except John, got a good laugh out of that. He had a frown on his face and seemed offended. "You know it's not that funny," he said seriously. "Brother Joe was in a scary situation."

Well, we stopped laughing immediately. Heck, we didn't realize it was such a big deal to him. Then, as we sat there feeling sorry for making a joke, John suddenly let a whoop and began laughing uncontrollably. The joke was on us.

"Brother John," I said after the laughter died down. "This was fun. The story was good, the fellowship was good, and the food was real good. But, unfortunately, we have to get going, so instead of sneaking out and sticking me with the lunch bill or telling me you forgot your wallet, give me your ticket, and I will pay. I have to say it was worth it this time."

"Well, that's awful, Brotherly of you, my Brother," John said as he waved one of the employees over. "Could you bring my lunch bill to my Brother Chris? He has graciously offered to pay for my lunch."

The employee smiled and said, "Mr. Deacon, every time you drive through Waco, you stop and eat here. Because of all the money you have spent here over the years, the manager told me to tell you that your meal today is on the house."

It was my turn to let out a whoop, and when I did, I looked over at John, and the look on his face as he realized that technically I was getting the free lunch by not having to pay for his was priceless. John's mouth was moving, but no words were coming out, and that is how we left him.

Yes sir! It was a great day!

At Capparelli's And Satisfaction In The Work

It's the same every month. John calls and says he is starving and wants to know where I am taking him to eat. Somehow he finds a way to make me pay. Well, it was about time for that to stop. John claims that good material is not free, and since I meet with him every month and write his words, I ought to be happy to buy his lunch. I am some of the time. The way he eats, a man could go bankrupt pretty quickly. It's only once a month, but it's the principle of the thing.

There was a new Italian restaurant named Capparelli Bros. we hadn't been to yet that I wanted to try. So, I told John I would meet him there and hurried to get there before he did. It's not a very big place, and I wanted to make sure we sat in the very back corner so when he got the crazies, as he usually does, that we would not be a spectacle. I was glad to see as I walked in that the table in the back was open. Tara, the owner, met me inside the door and told me to sit anywhere I wanted. I told her thanks and that I was going to the back table. I added that I hoped they cooked enough food today. Then, out of the corner of my eye, I saw the puzzled look on her face as I passed. I chuckled under my breath, knowing she wouldn't be puzzled long.

Our server was a lovely young lady who brought a couple of iced teas, some delicious bread, olive oil, and Italian spices while waiting for John, who was taking longer than I thought he would. I was starting to get a little worried when the door flew open, and he rushed in. Every person in the place turned to see what the commotion was, and for a split second, I thought about sliding down in my chair and hiding. But, instead, I waved, and he saw me and headed back to the table with all eyes on him.

When he slid into his seat, he had a sheepish look on his face, "I got lost. My darned navigation took me to the livestock feed store down the road, and I thought you were trying to be funny sending me there. So I went in looking for you to spoil the joke."

"I wasn't there, John," I said.

"I know that now," John said sarcastically. "I am about to die of hunger, so we need to eat now."

Tara arrived at our table to take our orders. She looked at me first. I ordered Lasagna and a small Caesar Salad. She smiled her approval of my choice and turned to John. As he began to order, at first, all seemed normal. John ordered the eggplant parmigiana and an Italian Salad. Once again, she smiled and reached for the menus. After taking mine, she reached for Johns, who refused to give it up. He just looked at her confused face and began to order more. Tara had filled one page on her pad and most of the next by the time he was done. John added an appetizer called tomato bread, a bowl of spaghetti and meatballs, a plate of lasagna, and two medium pizzas. When he was done and handed her the menu, Tara smiled at me, "Now I understand." I informed John that we were splitting the bill today, I was buying my lunch, and he was buying his. John smiled and nodded like he understood.

It wasn't long before we had our food, and with all John had ordered, there was not enough room on our table, so Tara left the serving tray on its stand next to the table with several of his dishes still on it. I could see other diners staring as a full plate replaced an emptied plate on the tray. We managed to get through the meal without incident except for the two older guys who came up and shook John's hand and told him they had never seen anyone eat that much at one sitting. I told them to stick around while he had dessert, and they had a good laugh as they left. I wasn't laughing, though. John had dessert, of course, and finally, I asked him if he wanted to share anything for this month's newsletter.

Instead of giving me a hard time, he got a far-off look on his face and smiled the smile of a contented man. (Heck, he ought to be content. He just ate enough to last him a week.) But I soon found out that his contentment was not because of a full belly but more being full of Masonry. "Are you going to just sit there with that goofy smile on your face?" I asked. "Or are you going to speak?" Usually, that would elicit a negative, sarcastic response from him, but for some strange reason, John was unfazed.

"Brother Chris," he said finally, that smile still on his face. "I don't know how it happens or why it happens, but it happens to me from time to time. I am sure it happens to a lot of Brothers. And when it happens to me, it's like a slow controlled explosion in my mind. When it happens, and I think about it, I have to smile cause it makes me feel darn good."

Dear Reader, I have to admit that right about here, I was close to losing my patience and began beating him vigorously, waiting for him to get to the point if... there was one.

John took a breath, and I waited; right then, Tara, God bless her heart, appeared to fill our tea glasses. "Thank you kindly, Darlin," John said, still smiling as she nodded and went to welcome another diner. And I continued to wait. Y'all know that waiting is not one of my strong suits.

Finally, John took another deep breath and began, "Brother Chris, I was sitting in my Lodge just the other night. I was not expecting to have one of those moments, but I did. We had an Entered Apprentice Degree scheduled for the evening, and everything was just beginning. I had picked a spot to watch the degree that was different from where I usually sit. As I sat there peering out from the darkness into the light (now the Brothers know where I was sitting), I watched something that truly made me feel good and made me smile. As I watched, I saw why I love coming to the Lodge. I saw what we are all supposed to see when we bring another good man into our gentle Fraternity. Watching my Brothers perform that night, I heard more than just the words of the ritual, and I saw more than just the movements of the ritual. I saw pride in the work, and I saw the love of the Fraternity. It occurred to me as I sat there that our work in the Lodge, all of it is so much more than just words and movements. We are, after all, teaching life lessons and moral and spiritual truths in a most effective and lasting way. We are teaching right from wrong and defining good from the bad. And when we perform our ritual, the words have to have feeling, and the movements have to have meaning. Then our lessons and our teachings start to make sense.

We tell all new Brothers that they got a *good degree*, but that is not always true. When they don't get that good degree, it's because there is no pride or love in the work. Many times, words are repeated by memory without any emotion. Movements were carried out haphazardly without regard to accuracy and all without any understanding of why. Sometimes Brothers are asked to perform certain parts of the ritual when they aren't ready or adequately prepared. At times a Brother will take on a role that he may think he is prepared for, but he is not, and again the candidate doesn't get that *good degree*.

I don't know if I can explain what I am talking about in the right way here, but I will try. A degree with only a few words missed or a movement not performed right is still considered good. However, when there is sincerity in their voice, happiness in their delivery, and love in their tone, that is something special and is, for the most part, a good degree for the candidate as he has no way of knowing if or what mistakes were made.

We need to understand that every degree, while it is put on for the benefit of the candidate, it is also for the benefit of the Brethren performing it as well as for those watching. There is a lifetime of lessons and life knowledge within each Masonic degree, and a candidate can only learn a very small amount during his actual ceremony. Most Brothers don't realize, and we don't impress upon them adequately, that to learn those secrets of life that all men say is a reason they desired Masonic membership, they need to continue to see the degrees performed as often as they can. They need to try to perform in the degrees. They need to be in a receptive and reflective frame of mind when performing or to watch a degree. As I found out the other night, it's enjoyable to watch a degree from a different place in the Lodge from time to time. When a Brother comes to a degree in the right frame of mind, the degree delivered with the appropriate respect, and the appropriate emotion, those slow explosions in the mind, those moments of unexpected realization, and those *wow* moments happen. That's when a Brother starts learning and understanding and uncovering the secrets he is searching for."

John paused to take a breath, and I jumped in, knowing the penalty for doing so, "But John, I have been to some degrees that the only thing I learned is that the Brothers doing the degree didn't seem to care about how it was done. They just wanted to get it over with."

"Ahh, yes, Brother Chris," he replied, surprisingly without sarcasm. "I, too, have sat in Lodges where there was no pride in the work. Also, I have sat there with a pain in my stomach, feeling sorry for the candidate who will come to realize that the Brethren of his Lodge cared little to give him the start in Masonry that he was promised and deserved. I have watched the Brethren who were members of the same Lodge, as they sat there and watched with pained looks of embarrassment on their faces, knowing that what was being performed was dismal. At the time, I couldn't help wondering why they allowed that kind of work to go on. I have to believe that every Mason has a burning desire to do things right. It is, after all, one of our most basic principles. Knowing that it is mind-boggling that a Lodge of Brothers wouldn't mandate that all work be done correctly and then put in the proper effort to practice and ensure high-quality work. Maybe they don't realize what a Mason should be, or maybe they don't care."

I saw the smile was gone now, and John had a sad look on his face. "I have seen the same things, John," I said. "I agree with your assessment. Tell me more about the other night."

As I hoped, the smile came back, and the sadness was gone, but unfortunately not forgotten. John got a far-off kind of gaze, not looking at anything, recalling the good feelings of that night and that degree, and said in not much more than a whisper, "It was one of those *wow* moments that lasted the whole evening. I could see the effort of the degree team as the result of their hard work in practice. They put their all into the ritual. I could hear the emotion and love transmitted in the words, and I could feel the lessons being taught as though I was the candidate again. It reminded us that God, the Supreme Architect of our Universe, is and should be the center of our lives. As mushy as this sounds....it was beautiful. And I can't wait for the next degree."

I watched as John reached up and brushed something from the corners of his eyes. What a softy he is. John then mumbled that he had to go to the restroom and quickly got up. I warned him as he walked away not to try to get out of the bill, and he shook his head. After a few minutes, I saw him return into the dining room and walk up to the front counter. He looked like he was paying his bill. I watched as he finished up and came back to the table. He stuck out his big paw and shook my hand, with that familiar grip, "Brother, I have to get on down the road. Those Big working tools don't sell themselves, you know." I told him to drive safe, and thanks for the talk.

As I sat there thinking about how great his story was, Tara came up and sat my bill on the table. I glanced at it, and my good feeling immediately turned to bad as I saw that John's bill was with mine. He hadn't paid his bill at all. I asked Tara what John was doing at the counter, and she said that he told her that it was his birthday and that he and I were Brothers. As mad as I was, all I could do was laugh out loud. It was true, and I could not deny it. We were, in fact, Brothers. Next month it's going to be different, I guarantee it!

CHESTER'S
HAMBURGERS

Beula, Gertrude, And The One And Only Chesters

This last month was bizarre in many ways, and it is a little painful to relive, but in some weird way, I needed to tell the story. If you are reading this, you are one of the ones that get to hear the whole story. I sent John and a few of those closest to him a slightly different version because, well, you will understand after you get done reading it. As most of you know, Davy Crockett Lodge conferred our 8th annual *Widows Degree* last month, and it was a great success, as were the previous seven. The Widows Degree was created to honor all wives and ladies of Masons and let everyone laugh at us Masons by presenting a ceremony in which we initiate the ladies of Masons into a "secret" …wink, wink…. sorority of Masonic Widows. Not Widows in the traditional sense, but widows as in hunting widows, football widows, or golf widows. To keep it fresh every year, we tweak it slightly and add or subtract a small part, always keeping the main body of the program intact. It is always a super funny program, and everyone has a load of fun.

This year the Brothers talked me into dressing as an older woman and portraying a member of the Grand Council of the Organization to confer the degree. At first, I wanted nothing to do with that idea, but I was reminded that our Brother Brad had dressed in drag the year before, and everyone loved it. -Soooo, reluctantly, I agreed to become Ms. Beula Mae Beanblossom with the stipulation that we would keep it secret from everyone until I was introduced in the degree. Little did I know that Brad was going to surprise everyone and become Gertrude Shufflebottom once again. We sent out all the advertisements for the degree and started getting

RSVPs back. Now, that is all the background I am going to give before I tell the story.

A couple of days before the night of the Widows Degree, John called and said he had a big sales meeting in Houston and would be spending the night in San Antonio on Tuesday before continuing to Houston the next morning. He wanted to meet for dinner and talk about the article for September. I told him that I couldn't because of the Widows program that night, but I talked him into coming to Lodge and watching the program. I told him we would try to meet before for a few minutes.

When John arrived that night, I greeted him. We talked for a short time, but I couldn't spend much time with him because, not being used to dressing like a woman and knowing it would take a while, I had to disappear early to get it done. I told him I would meet him for lunch the next day and we could talk about the article. John knew a lot of the Brothers at our Lodge, and he knew Pam, so I wasn't worried about leaving him alone. I also warned him about his behavior since I would have my Daughter with me at lunch, who was visiting from Oregon.

As it turned out, the degree went fine, and everyone had a great time. We initiated 21 new Masonic Widows with the usual ceremonies. I looked for John afterward but couldn't find him. Pam told me that he had told her he was tired and went to the hotel to sleep.

The next morning, I called him and set up lunch at a place called Chester's hamburgers. We may have eaten there before, but I had a taste for a green chili cheeseburger, and Chester's has the best. As usual, John was there before Brenda, and I got there, and, boy, was he in a great mood. That sent up a red flag in my mind, and I hoped he wasn't going to get us banned from this place.

Brenda and I found him in a back booth behind a large menu. We sat there listening to him talking to himself for a couple of minutes before realizing we were there. I introduced John to Brenda and gave him a warning glare which he ignored while good-naturedly bashing me for her benefit. Ordering food at Chester's requires you to go to the counter and make your order and pay. Of course, realizing this, John had found a place to sit, and he waited till I got there before ordering. I told him and Brenda that we might as well go and order. I had to jump back to keep from getting trampled by John, who ensured he was first in line.

Brenda ordered some kind of salad. As she ordered, John gave her a weird look, asking her why she was having rabbit food for lunch. He then proceeded to order what seemed like one of everything on the menu. John ordered two of my favorite green chili cheeseburgers, a regular chili con carne burger, and enough fries and onion rings to feed a normal person for a week. I thought I heard him tell the cashier that his Brother was paying as he stepped down the counter to pick up his drink…wow what a surprise. I ordered a green chili cheeseburger and my own fries cause heaven forbid John would offer any of his to anyone else. When I finally got to the table, John conversed with Brenda and waited for my name. I was pretty sure when that happened; I wouldn't be the one rushing up to the counter to get our food. I just hoped he didn't eat much, walking back to the table.

True to form, when they called out Chris on the speaker, John was there to pick up our tray in a flash. I watched closely as he walked back to the table and made sure that the fries he stole on the walk were the ones he took off the tray for himself.

I learned something that day. John usually never talks when he eats, or so I thought. John and my Daughter carried on a running conversation the whole time they ate like she was talking to *Uncle John* or something. He just dug in like he hadn't eaten in a week, and he kept talking the whole time. John talked to Brenda and me and sometimes to no one in particular. Then something bizarre happened. As he talked, he began to talk about the Widows Degree the night before. Brenda was one of the only ones that knew I was dressing up as Beula Mae. John talked about how much he liked the program and said that he couldn't find me to say goodbye after the program. Then, as he was babbling along about the Widows Program, right in the middle of a bite of my hamburger, he said plain as day, "Now don't you ever tell Mrs. Deacon I said this but, Boy, that Beula Mae sure is a looker, yup, and Gertrude wasn't bad either."

I thought, oh my God, as an electric shock went up to my spine!! I choked and jerked my head up, and at the same time, a little chunk of French fry shot out of my mouth right past a still babbling John. Thank goodness he never saw it. I heard Brenda choke and cough next to me, and our eyes met in horror, both of us struggling not to laugh out loud. John not only didn't see the missile I launched at him but lucky for us, he never caught on to mine and Brenda's emotional and physical distress. Brenda couldn't stand it and ran for the Ladies' room. I was still choking and coughing. John looked up and asked if I was all right. And I have to admit that this is one of those times that you have to lie to a Brother. I told him I was fine when I wasn't. I told him if he ever mentioned that about another woman again…. especially those two, that I WOULD tell Mrs. Deacon. John shook his head and went back to eating, and then, I laughed, and I laughed and laughed. I couldn't stop, and John just shook his head sadly like I was having some kind of attack or something and ate in silence.

Brenda came back to the table with a strained look on her face. Brenda announced that she had to go and gave John and me a hug. Out the door, she went. I saw that John was finishing up and asked if he had anything for the newsletter.

He took a long swallow from his iced tea, leaned back," Yes, I have something for you. I have been concerned about something for a long time, Brother Chris. It's about guys complaining that their wives don't like Masonry. They say they have a bad opinion about the Fraternity or don't have any interest in being a part of it or assisting their husbands in it. And this topic is a very sticky subject, so I will have to be real diplomatic here because I don't want to upset anyone."

"Yup," I said with a laugh. "Diplomacy has not ever been your strong suit."

"That's not a very nice thing to say," John growled…but went on anyway. "Like I was saying, this is not the easiest of topics, but I think it's something that needs to be addressed for both the Masons as well as the ladies. You have to realize and tell your readers that this is just one old cowpoke's opinion. And you know what they say about opinions; they are like a……."

"Hey, now," I said, holding up my hand for him to stop. "I can't print that, and you know it."

"OK… OK… sorry," he said apologetically as I shook my head at him. "I just get to talking, and stuff just comes out."

"I will make sure everyone knows it's your opinion," I promised. "But let's get after it cause I don't have all day." That got me a John Deacon glare, but he finally began talking again.

"In my opinion, if a woman is just not interested in assisting her husband or being a part of his Masonic journey, then he shouldn't worry about it, nor should he try to force her to. If she is comfortable with his membership as a Mason and allows his level of participation, then she should be allowed her space. However, those ladies of ours who have a dislike for our Fraternity possibly due to a lack of understanding of Masonry or because they resent the time that our Masonic duties take away from them and the family that I am going to try to offer some light and understanding. Before you state the obvious and remind me that there are hardly any women who read your newsletter, what I am going to say is the same whether a lady or a Brother is reading it. Hopefully, some Brothers will read this and either get a Masonic lady to read it or, at the very least, maybe gain some understanding himself that will help him with a lady who has misgivings or even outright hostility towards the Craft.

First, let's define what Masonic involvement is for a wife or lady of a Mason. There IS NO involvement in a real sense. Women cannot be Masons in our Grand jurisdiction, and they cannot sit in Lodge meetings, nor can they participate in any business related to the Lodge. The extent of their involvement is that of attending open meetings and family programs. Knowing this, I believe that what we desire from our ladies is not so much involvement but rather acceptance and encouragement from them. But let's look at the situation logically; you tell her that you are joining a Lodge and that it is for men only and that its purpose is to make good men better men, and it is a system of moral development. Then you tell her that you will be initiated into three degrees and that you don't know anything about the degrees. After your first initiation, when you know what is in the degree, you inform her you can't tell her anything about it because.... *IT'S A SECRET.*

Then you tell her that you will have to study with an instructor a couple of times a week and go to a couple of Lodge meetings a month. But you can't tell her what you are studying, except it's no big deal cause it's a *SECRET*. Do you know what she hears? She only hears, 'I am going to join a Lodge, and I am going to spend a lot of time doing stuff without you that I can't tell you anything about.' When you look at it like this, I think it is easy to understand why a wife might have a few concerns."

"Oh wow, John," I blurted out without thinking. "Until you said all of that, I never realized how bad we screw this up with our wives."

"Yes, we do," he agreed. "But it's not all our fault. What Masonry is and what it means is hard enough for a veteran Brother to explain, much less for a brand new Brother. Brother Masons sometimes, more than I care to think about, never learn enough about the Craft to be able to explain it adequately to anyone, and certainly their wife. It's the word *secret* that causes the problems. I shudder to think how many of our Ladies have lived with their Husband/Mason for years without a proper understanding of the Lodge and what Masons do there. They are unhappy and barely tolerating something that has violated the promise we all make to our wives that there will be no secrets. Surely there is a point in which that promise, that perceived breach of trust, causes irreparable damage to a relationship that should have been made stronger and happier because of the beautiful lessons and principles of the Masonic Fraternity.

I am not saying that Masonic membership causes divorce, but I suspect, and I believe that many Brothers have dropped out either partially or entirely due to their wives not being able to understand or not wanting to wait for an understanding of what Masonry is and its true purpose. How many of our loving wives have we imposed years of feelings of uncertainty and uneasiness and maybe a little jealousy as we have happily traveled our Masonic journey, totally oblivious of the scars we may have created due to the difference between perception and truth.

Masonry takes hold of our hearts and minds, opening doors and casts aside veils within each of us. It causes us to sometimes, for the first time in our lives, to feel feelings that before were suppressed and to stir awakenings and discoveries in our character and to show us things about ourselves that we never knew before. Learning the work and the lessons of the three degrees brings a powerful sense of accomplishment. Those newly found feelings and sublime truths first discovered lead to greater confidence and a sense of well-being, which should naturally translate into a better and happier man. But many times, the opposite happens. The hurt created by the perception that the man is embarking alone on a secret and separate life and his obvious love and attachment to this life could make a wife withdraw and create a divide between them. Sometimes this is obvious and sometimes not, but it is always there...."

John paused to take a drink from his glass, and my mind began to wander. As I pondered, I began to wonder how much hurt I had caused, how blind I could have been to the obvious. Listening to John was a revelation for sure. "Oh my God, John, I whispered. "We have really screwed this up big time."

"Yes," he replied. "We surely have, and it may be big-time like you said and for some maybe not as bad as we think, but whatever the level, it's not good. But how do we fix it, Brother Chris? How can we possibly make them understand that this love for Freemasonry is not a substitute for the love of a wife and family. It can never be a replacement for the lifelong companionship of a wife.

On the contrary, freemasonry aims to enhance his relationships and ultimately lead to a happier man who makes those around him happier. How can we comfort them with the fact that the perceived secrets are just that perceived? They are necessary to the search, and that the real Masonic secrets relate to something much more profound and something much more important that is found within each of us. Can we ever succeed in showing them that Masonry is the vehicle that unlocks those deeper characteristics of a man's inner self and allows the real him to step into the light of moral and spiritual truth? How will they ever believe that this journey could never be complete or even be possible without the love of that remarkable woman…. a wife…. a friend ….and a companion.

We have a lot of work to do, my Brother. So spread the word…. we have much work to do!"

WHATABURGER AND A LOT MORE THAN MAKING GOOD MEN BETTER

Over the years of my friendship with John Deacon, we have covered a lot of topics. Some topics we have covered and continue to cover from several different angles. I have learned much from him, and he gives me a lot to think about. There is no doubt that at least the one time of the month that we meet and talk about Masonry, he fully inserts himself into my life, and I guess to some degree, his influence is present most of the rest of the time.

It is hard to prepare for my monthly visit with John because he sometimes shows up without warning. Such was the case this month. It was Monday before last, and we were having a cool spell, which in South Texas in the fall means high temperatures in the 90's instead of the 100's. I was at my desk at the counter, which faces the front of the building. The whole front of the shop is a series of large windows facing the parking lot, and nothing can enter or leave without Roger and I seeing it. John kind of showed up all of a sudden. We heard him a couple of seconds before we saw him. A big black Ford F-350, sputtering and misfiring pretty bad, pulled up to our front door, followed by a massive cloud of black smoke. I heard Roger mutter under his breath, "Who in the world is this?" Whoever was inside turned off the motor, and as the smoke began to clear, I could see a rather large cowboy, obviously in a state of distress, behind the wheel. "That's your crazy friend John and that truck he calls Blackie," Roger said, shaking his head.

John just sat there in his truck like he expected us to run out and wait on him in the parking lot. There was no way that I was going out there. John loves that truck and considers it a part of the family, and anytime anything happens to it, he becomes the biggest drama queen. I preferred dealing with it all from a sitting position in the cool of my office. As we sat there watching, and with great effort, John slowly dragged himself out of the truck. We saw him reach out and lay his hand on the front fender as if offering some comfort to an ailing friend. I heard Roger mumble, "My God, more than likely, all he needs is a fuel filter. He probably hasn't changed it in forever."

"I agree, but as much grief as I have to endure from John, let's have a little fun with him before we let him off the hook." Roger chuckled and nodded his head as John walked in the door.

John walked up to the counter in front of me and, in a voice that sounded a little quivery, "Brother Chris, you have to help Blackie. He's a hurtin bad. I am afraid it's not good."

"Well, good morning to you too, Brother John, and what a fine day it is too."

"Brother Chris," John whined. "Blackie is sitting out there in front of your shop in an obvious state of sickness and distress, and all you can do is make jokes. Have you no feelings at all?" Just then, Roger bolted out the door to the shop, and I couldn't tell if it was to laugh out loud or to lose his breakfast.

I got one of my technicians to take Blackie to the back and check it out. I told John that we might go have something to eat while we waited for the diagnosis. If you can believe it, John was real hesitant to leave that danged truck. "Don't be ridiculous, John," I said disgustingly. "This is no hospital, and that truck is not alive, so cut it out." I immediately felt terrible because he looked like he might cry. "Come on, John," I said a little softer. "Let's run up to Whataburger and get us a hamburger, or two, or three, and it will be better when we get back." Reluctantly John followed me out to my truck and climbed in.

He was totally quiet on the short trip down the road to the Whataburger. I actually believe that whatever ails a big juicy Whataburger can cure you. I feel sorry that the rest of the world doesn't have Whataburger. It's just one more reason I thank the Great Architect every day that I live in Texas. John acted surprised when I pulled into the drive-through, and as I pulled up to the menu board, I told him, "I come here a lot of days for lunch by myself, and I get my food and sit here in my truck and eat. I get a lot of good thinking done that way."

John smiled, "Because I am on the road all the time, I do the same, and I am not too proud to say that I am pretty much addicted to most everything on the menu."

What a revelation, I thought as the speaker crackled with the familiar voice of Becky, the drive-through girl. "What'll it be today sir," she asked in her usual chipper voice? "I have a rider today," I replied. "So I am going to need a couple of minutes to check the menu." "Let me know when you are ready," she answered.

I turned to John and immediately knew something was wrong. He was staring at the menu like it was printed in a foreign language. "What's wrong John," I asked.

"It's gone," is all he would say.

"What's gone?"

"The Sweet and Spicy Bacon Burger is gone," John said with obvious emotion in his voice. God bless Becky because she heard him, and she said, "The picture is gone, but we've still got it." Well, that made him happy, and he began to order. He ordered two Sweet and Spicy Bacon Burgers, an Avocado Bacon Burger, all with fries and jalapenos, and a drink. I ordered my usual Patty melt meal, and before I told her we were done, John added three lemon pies. I finally told Becky we were done and moved up to the window to pay. Before I stopped, John informed me that he would pay, but he left his wallet on Blackie's seat. Heck, I wasn't even listening; this wasn't my first rodeo.

Becky commented that I must be feeding the whole shop. I gestured towards John, "Nope, only him." She leaned out the window towards my truck and gave John a once-over look, and said to me in a low voice, "Heck, Chris, this might only be a snack for him." I laughed and agreed. I pulled up to the second window to get our food. John was trying to get me to tell him what Becky said as the window opened, but Jerry, the assistant manager, poked his head out and said hi. They must be able to talk to each other on those headsets because he was already laughing as he glanced past me at John. I heard John snort when Jerry asked me if I needed him to double bag my order or if I wanted it all at once or in shifts. John leaned over and said, "Keep the fire hot cause we'll be back for the second course in a minute." Jerry's face went blank, and I waved as we drove away.

I found a cool parking place next to a shade tree to eat. My cell phone rang just as I finished. Roger let me know that they found the fuel filter was long past its regular service time, and after it was changed, the truck ran great. I thanked him and thought for a second about messing with John, but I told him the truth. Finally, his stress seemed to melt away. When he took the last bite of his last lemon pie, John sat back and took a deep breath, "Well, I am ready to talk now if you want to hear it."

"Well, that's a surprise," I answered. "Usually, I have to beg."

"Not today, my Brother. Blackie is good to go, and my belly is full. The only thing that is keeping me from a nice nap is talking to you, so let's get to it."

"Ok then, I already spent half my weekly allowance feeding you; this better be good."

"How about this," John began. "I got blindsided by my granddaughter last week."

I was puzzled, "What do you mean blindsided?"

"My six-year-old granddaughter, Hailey, climbed up on the couch next to me, and just out of nowhere, she asked, 'Papaw, why do you love the Lodge so much?' That hit me kinda hard because after I answered her, I couldn't stop thinking about it."

"What did you say to her, John?"

"Well, I answered way too quickly and told her that it was because it made me a better person. She looked at me and said, 'But Papaw, you are already a better person.'"

"Wow," I whispered. "I'll bet that got to you. She pretty much made your day, huh?"

"She sure did," he replied. "I gave her a big hug and had to wipe the corners of my eyes and told her I loved her very, very much, but I still couldn't get her question out of my mind. Later after thinking about it pretty hard, I realized that my answer was true enough, but it was also vague and incomplete. I didn't mean for it to be, but that old cliché about making us better men is used way too much as an easy way out when we don't have an answer or don't care to give one."

"So now that you have thought about it, what would you say differently," I asked, eager to hear more?

"I have thought about it," John began. "If a non-mason or even my wife were to ask me why I loved the Lodge or Masonry so much, I think I would have to tell them how it has made me feel.

I still remember the night of my first initiation. By the time that evening was done, I knew in my mind and my heart that I had just become a part of something much bigger than myself. Freemasonry is so big and so good that I was overwhelmed by its greatness and beauty. I honestly went home that first night a different man, the same, but different inside. As beautiful and enlightening as the degrees were, I could feel deep down inside that there was much more than the degrees were only a part of the whole. As time went on and I learned more, I found myself asking questions and seeking answers. Over time and by using the lessons I learned in the degrees, I found myself searching within myself for the answers to some of those questions. When I did that, I discovered things about myself that I never knew before. I found a renewed relationship with God. I found a deeper understanding of what makes me....me. With that understanding came some clarity, and I now know that with knowledge and clarity comes harmony and happiness. And that harmony and happiness make me a better man.

You have to understand that this doesn't happen to every man, nor does it necessarily occur fast in those that it does happen to. But I can say that it has happened to me, and I believe it happens to most Masons in varying degrees depending on how each receives and understands the lessons given him. Within the Lodge, the structure is an atmosphere of sharing and giving, an atmosphere of encouragement, an atmosphere without ridicule or criticism. Suppose you add to that, Brotherly love. In that case, you find that a man has a wonderful opportunity, with a clear mind, to learn and grow and focus on building, reinforcing, and strengthening his character and then applying that knowledge and those lessons to the outside world and his everyday life. This is the power that has changed societies and built nations throughout history. This is the power of good, and this is the power of Freemasonry.

That is what most Masons do behind the closed doors of their Lodge buildings in those so-called *secret* meetings. This is what we need to communicate to all non-Masons and all Masons' families. Telling people this does not violate any of our obligations to keep our esoteric work secret and exclusive and private things to us. I realize that it is hard and, in some cases, impossible to explain that all the esoteric secrets are meaningless unless they are learned as part of the Masonic ritual process. But we all know that without the ritual, those words are just words. The ritual, together with the explanation of the lessons in Masonry, gives the words their power and meaning."

John paused, and in the brief silence that followed, my mind embraced what he had just said. I thought about all the times I wished I could have said what I just heard to someone who made some smart alec comment about Masonry or just wanted to know more than the usual, *we make good men better explanation.* "That's very good, John," I said. "You took my mind back to a very good place."

"But I have not finished telling you why I love the Lodge as much as I do," John said. "Before I do, I have to say something that every Mason should communicate to their families. Every Brother should tell their wives and their families that, as beautiful and as important as the lessons and philosophy of Masonry are, it is not taught anywhere in Masonry that the Craft comes before Mason's family. The family always comes before the Craft or should. Any Brother who believes differently or conducts his life differently hasn't learned his lessons well.

The real reason I love Lodge and Masonry so much is my Brothers. I could receive the degrees of Masonry in a Lodge and never return and spend my life reading and researching and learning and practicing the lessons of Masonry and live an excellent Masonic life in every respect. I don't need the Lodge to do that. But it is the Brothers that make Masonry what it is for me, and I believe that is true for most Brothers. I love Masonry for what it is and what it does for me and what it has done for all Masons and this world, but my association with all those men who I call my Brothers makes it special.

Men who I can trust and who trust me. Men who would lay down their life for me or any other Brother and for the cause of good men who would see that my family was taken care of in the event of my death. Men who have my best interests at heart because we are Brothers. There is nothing that I wish for myself that I don't wish for my Brothers, but given all of that, our families are foremost, and we should tell them that because sometimes it may appear to them otherwise. So, Brother Chris, is your family more important than Masonry? Does your family know that they are more important than the Craft to you?"

I was following along and enjoying his words and not prepared for the questions. Finally, I realized I was silent for too long. I opened my mouth, and nothing came out. Finally, my mind caught up with my mouth and, "Of course they are more important, but I- I- I don't know if they know it…. I mean, I think they do, but I don't know for sure."

"Well, maybe you need to tell them, my Brother. You know that we are all guilty of taking things for granted. We get married, and we relax and take our wives for granted. We stop communicating, and we don't give it a second thought, just like we initiate a new Entered apprentice, and we take them for granted too. We think that they are Masons now, and beyond the memory work, we stop communicating with them, helping them, and teaching them about Masonry. Both our Families and our Brothers are an ongoing proposition, and neither should ever be neglected."

John stopped, and I realized I was late getting back to the shop. So I cranked the truck up and began the trip back. Like the trip up, there was no conversation on the way back, but for a different reason. Once again, I learned a valuable lesson from the big guy. I definitely needed to do some things, and I was unhappy with myself for not making sure it was done. But, John was thrilled to get his truck back. He gave me a big hug and roared out of the parking lot with a big grin on his face.

I know I have a lot of work to do. I suspect y'all do too.

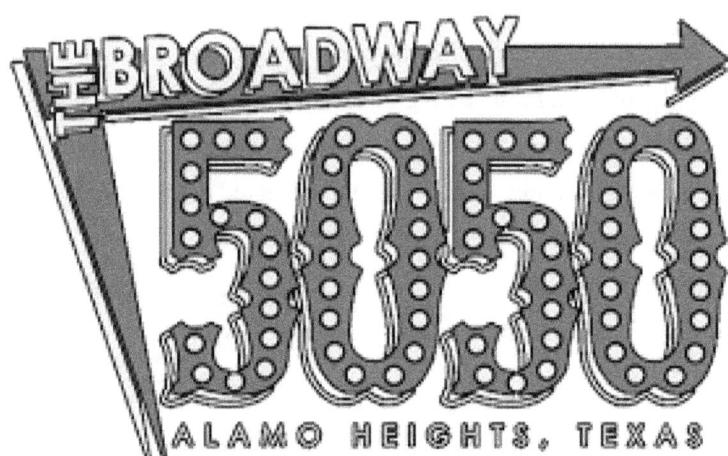

THE BROADWAY 5050
ALAMO HEIGHTS, TEXAS

A LITTLE 50/50 AND THERE IS MEANING IN EVERYTHING

It was just another hot, muggy, and, yes, humid South Texas day in late October. Pam was gone to get her nails, all twenty of them, done. I was at home with my hound dog and my thoughts. I was getting ready to go do something I had meant to do for a while. The phone rang, and when I answered, it made me smile because having the company of my Brother John Deacon was just what this errand called for. Before he could say anything, I told him to meet me for lunch and gave him the address.

The address I gave him belonged to a tiny eatery called the Broadway 50/50, which coincidentally corresponded to 5050 Broadway in the Alamo Heights 1909 part of San Antonio. The building had been there by most historical accounts since the mid-1920s. My interest in it was that my Lodge met in a room on the second floor of that building in its early years. The Worshipful Master had expressed an interest in obtaining permission to use the room for one special night to meet informally as members of the Lodge and experience the atmosphere of the building where our earliest Lodge members met and take in a bit of history. I was immediately on board with the idea, but before presenting it to the Brethren, I first needed to obtain that permission, which was today's object.

Not surprisingly, John beat me there (it was all about food for him after all). As I entered, I could hear his booming voice chastising Amy and her waitress trainee Janie about the virtues of having Chicken Fried Steak in every Texas restaurant and the fact that there was none on the menu before him. They seemed to be taking it all in stride but also close to smacking him. I squeezed myself into the booth across from John, realizing suddenly that all of the booths I sit in with him seem to have less room on my side than his; go figure. The girls left to get our beverages while we got our heys and how's it goins out of the way. When they returned, we were ready to order, and John began as usual.

Now I need to throw in here that I had been battling a severe case of allergies to mold and dust lately, and it had all ended up clogging up my lungs. I was in the middle of a bottle of steroid pills to help clear it all out. Well, I am not a big pill taker, but these darn things cranked my energy up by double, and aside from getting a lot more things done than usual, it makes me powerfully hungry; all the time. So when John ordered a basket of fried pickles, I said, "me too" from behind my menu. There was a pause before John continued by ordering two hamburgers, an El Jefe and a Mushroom Swiss Burger to which I held up my hand and chimed in, "me too and me too." An even longer silence followed, and I cou"d feel John's eyes"staring at my menu's other side, which I dropped d"wn to just below e"e level. I could see the girls out of the corner of my eye grinning at John's confusion. He stared for a few more seconds and then said, "Add an order of onion rings to mine, Darlin," to which I announced, "me too."

With that, John rolled his eyes, shook his head, closed the menu, and said, "That's it, I hope." I could still hear those girls giggling as they disappeared into the kitchen to place our order. John just continued to glare at me, confused, until I finally told him what was happening. I had asked Amy to talk to the manager, and he finally came over, thinking I wanted to complain about something. I invited him to sit on my side where there was room and proceeded to tell him the story of my Lodge and its history in the building. He was fascinated by what I told him but sadly for me and, as he assured me, for him also, that the building had been damaged by a fire a couple of years before. While the building was structurally sound, the upstairs was by order of the Fire Marshall and city engineers, off-limits to anyone but the owners, and was being used for light storage. He apologized and offered to let us use the lower main room for our purpose, but because he had no understanding of our intentions, I thanked him and declined. Finally, our lunch showed up, and John immediately fell silent and attacked after sliding plates strategically towards him.

I was thankful for several reasons. I was starving because of the drugs and had plenty to eat, and I was going to eat it all. Also, I was disappointed in the outcome of our idea and just needed some time to get right with it. As we ate, I began to think about some of the things I had heard over the years about the Lodge's time here in this old building. I had read minutes from meetings from that period in our Lodges history, and it wasn't hard to imagine being there in that room on a dark Tuesday night in the mid-1940s. There is something about a Masonic Lodge meeting that no matter how many you have attended or where they are all the same, they are all different and unique for all kinds of different reasons. Because of that, you can be there in every one of them, whether you were or not. With a smile, I recalled the story of when there was a ladies' lingerie shop on the ground floor when the Lodge met above, and that one night, the plumbing failed in the Lodge and subsequently flooded the ladies shop below. The Brethren of the Lodge all got together to help with the clean-up. Many stepped up and bought most of the items that were destroyed. It is said that several of the Brothers were duly chastised by their wives and served dog house time for purchasing as much as they did. Masons, albeit good men, are still just men. While I was daydreaming, without realizing it, I had finished all my food. However, I couldn't be sure looking at the table, but it looked like my onion rings had possibly made their way into John's bottomless pit.

John sat there with an innocent look on his face as the mountain of trash was being cleared away. I realized I needed to take advantage of this time to get something out of John to write my article for the month.

"You ate my onion rings," I said matter of factually. "You better have something good for this month."

John took a big drink of his iced tea followed by a deep breath, and began to talk without any admission. The more he spoke, the more excited he got.

"Brother Chris, one of the things I love about Masonry is the way it makes me think about all kinds of things. Things that are said every day, things I see or that happen to me, and even to other people every day almost always makes me take a second or two to ask myself, *what does that mean?* Those questions lead to a lot of interesting answers and many times more interesting questions. These are things that most people ignore, or it never dawns on them because they are not thinking that way. Masonry taught me to think beyond the obvious and look behind what is seen to what is unseen. Sounds weird and creepy, huh? But it is really not. It is just a frame of mind. And those *oh wow* moments keep on coming for me. Do you know what I am talking about?"

Well, my mind was spinning. Partly because of watching all he had just eaten and partly because of what I had just eaten, and partly because I wasn't sure what the heck John was saying. He was so animated I thought he might levitate out of his chair, but I figured by the laws of physics, a whole lot of weight + extra weight X gravity ÷ common sense = no possible levitation. "What in the Sam Hill are you talking about, John," I demanded? "I am getting a headache here. I get the gist of what you are talking about, but I just don't get where you are going with this." I was having a wow moment of my own. This was the most words I have gotten to say in forever talking to him.... woo hooo!!

"Ok..Ok, " John said, still excited. "It's like when someone says 'You can lead a horse to water, but you can't make him drink.' This is something you can relate to a lot of people and especially a lot of Masons. And it applies to almost everything. I have a few (unfortunately too few) Brothers with whom I can talk Masonry and Masonic philosophy. I hear them saying how they can't understand how a Brother, after going through the degrees, can't seem to grasp the concept of relating Masonic lessons and teachings to more than the basic and obvious meanings that are explained outright in the degree. Hell, they can't see the forest for the trees....... Ha, ha, did you hear that? I just used another one, and this also applies to just what we are talking about."

With my head still spinning a little, I said, "I see now where you are going, but what got you started on this and, more importantly, why?"

"Well, you are probably going to laugh when I tell you this," John said with a chuckle. "But I was sitting in a customer's office one-day last week, and when he came walking in, I saw he was wearing cowboy boots, and he had his pants tucked into the tops of the boots. I don't know if I ever told you this, but my Dad was an old cowboy who grew up on an old-time cattle ranch, and when I was a young boy, he told me once to 'never trust a man who stuffs his pants legs down into the tops of his boots.' All my life, I never thought too much about it or if it had some kind of meaning. I just took it at face value and usually just laughed about it. But as I sat there grinning inside, remembering his words, it dawned on me that there might be a message he was trying to convey. After our meeting, as I was heading to my next stop, I put some more thought into it. When I got back close to a computer, I asked Uncle Google About it and what I found out made me eager to find out more about all those other seemingly meaningless sayings that we were all told by our elders as kids. After just a couple of minutes of searching, I found out that some cowboys tuck their pants legs inside their pants in certain riding situations, such as riding in the brush. That didn't fly for my Dad cause he always said that's what chaps were for. But I realized that the message he was trying to convey to me was something that many old-time cowboys believed (and my Dad was one) that tucking the pant legs inside the boots is the mark of a show-off or a braggart or someone looking for attention. I realized that he was trying to tell me to watch out for someone who was possibly not a straight shooter, maybe a pretender. Immediately when I realized that, my mind related it to a phrase in our Entered Apprentice obligation that cautions us all to make sure that all our communications are the proper information to the proper recipient. Realizing all of that meant a lot to me. And it made me start to take a closer look at all those other *crazy things* he used to say.

"Ok," I said. "That's the how, but what about the why?"

"Well dang," Brother Chris, I feel really blessed having the ability and desire to take a wider and deeper look at things which my lessons in the Craft have taught me and, well, I am actually one of those Masons who wonder why some guys don't seem to get it. I wish they could all experience those wow moments too. I wonder why they don't and wonder if it just hasn't kicked in for them yet. So I thought if I could talk about some of my Dad's and others' old crazy sayings, maybe I could get some Brothers interested in sliding back that veil that separates the obvious from the hidden. But I wasn't sure you could relay it as understandable as I am saying to you now."

I had briefly looked down as he was talking, and when he said that last part, my head shot up, and I know my expression was a combination of confusion and anger at the same time, "What do you mean understandable," I demanded? "Do you think that my newsletter is all about you? I have to dress up and make understandable a lot of what you say, big boy. So you need to take a couple of steps down off my rear end.

John threw back his head and let out a huge laugh. "Just checking to see if you were paying attention, my Brother," he said, wiping tears out of his eyes. "One small correction, though; you may have to dress up a word of mine here and there, but it's the way I say them that makes this column what it is."

It was my turn to laugh a little. "Let "e tell you something, my triple extra-large brother," I said sarcastically. "Without me, there wouldn't even be a column."

"Don't flatter yourself," John shot back with a grin. "I could pull anyone off the street to do a better job writing this than you do."

Aha, I had him now, "You might be able to do that, but they sure as heck wouldn't be buying lunch for you and three of your hidden buddies every time you meet."

John smiled, and with a thoughtful look on his face, "Touché, my Brother. Now, do you want to hear the rest of my story?" I just shrugged, and he went on like he didn't notice. Amy had appeared at the table with our bill and I unconsciously (like it mattered anyway) slid my credit card to her to pay. "Like I was trying to tell you before, I was hoping to relate some everyday sayings to our Masonic lessons to illustrate how Masonry is all about life and moral behavior. I want to start with that 'can't see the forest for the trees' saying because we hear that the true Secrets of life are right in front of us. We have to prepare our minds to be able to see them. We go around every day in our lives, and too many times we are focused on the big picture, and we fail to recognize the little and the obvious things."

"I can see that, John," I replied.

"It is hard though in this fast-paced world to focus sometimes on the little things, but you are right; we need to." "How about this one," John continued. "One of the craziest (actually not really) things he always said was 'Never trust a man who chokes up on a hammer.'"

That made me laugh, "I don't see how that could be interpreted to allude to any serious moral message John," I replied, shaking my head.

"You know, I didn't think so either," John said with a chuckle, but the more I thought about it, it seemed to me that there was, in fact, a message there. To me, it seemed that he was talking about our working tools. Maybe he was talking about using tools the way they were intended in order to get the most work done. But, as it relates to real life, it also offers a gentle message to us Masons that in order for us to be able to make the positive changes in our characters we need to not only use the working tools that we have been given but also to use them the way they were intended to be used. At least it makes a lot of sense to me."

"I see what you mean," John, I said, starting to catch on. "Hey, maybe your Dad meant also that if you had to choke up on that hammer that you might lack confidence or trust in either yourself or the tool, and he was pointing that out. Do you have any more?"

"Well, there was this one he used to say all the time," I said cautiously.

"Tell me what it was."

"Well, anytime I would say 'I wish'... he would say (and I am going to sanitize his word a little) 'wish in one hand and poop in the other and see which one weighs more."

"That's a little rough, Brother Chris," he replied slowly, choosing his words carefully. "But it still teaches a lesson, I think. To me, it says that wishing is not reality and that wishing doesn't get anything done. But if it is something worthwhile, you need to formulate a plan to make it happen. Do you think that's it?"

I shook my head, "Nope, cause when he said it to me, it just meant I wasn't getting whatever it was."

John just stared at me with a blank look. "Brother Chris, I think you are starting to lose the point of this exercise. It's to find those meanings...."

"Oh yeah, well, maybe he was talking about the difference between thinking about doing something and actually getting it done," I offered.

"Good one," exclaimed John. "That might relate to that part of our third degree where a few fellers wanted something they weren't entitled to receive. It also relates to not following the rules. Just like that situation in our ritual when we just desire something, knowing we have not put forth the proper effort or followed the proper rules. What we get back is quite likely little or nothing representative of that deposit, in the other hand your Dad was talking about."

"I guess it's a possibility he was trying to impart a bigger message," I smiled unconvincingly. "But I am positive he was also letting me know I wasn't getting what I wanted. It is pretty cool, though, how many of the things we brush off as unimportant are actually big teaching moments. It shows the power of our Masonic teaching system that we can relate them to our lives so vividly."

"Dang, My Brother," John said, nodding his head in agreement as Amy slid my card back to me and mouthed the words "thanks" before heading to another table. "That's what I am talking about. What something says to me might not be exactly what it says to you or any other person. We are all different, and we all have different personal journeys. But, it's all about having that frame of mind that you are traveling on that journey to more light or knowledge to make yourself a better man and by your actions influence others. My Lord Brother Chris, that is what we are here to do!"

"That's a great Masonic lesson John," I replied as we headed for our vehicles. "It's a different way to think about it, and it gives perspective. It is amazing how you can take these and other sayings that people have said for ages and that we laugh at them because they sound funny and seemingly have no meaning at all, and relate them to everyday life or everyday people and realize how they also relate to our Masonic lessons. That's neat.

I remember our Worshipful Master telling a story about how he was cut off by a rude driver on his way home one day. While he was angrily stewing about it, he drove by a house being built. The workers were installing the roof. He watched them hammer the nails in the shingles; suddenly, it reminded him of the gavel, one of our principle working tools. He remembered how we are to divest or let go of those things that we know we need to get rid of to help us make our character stronger. These lessons and principles are instilled inside every mason, but they remain dormant until a man chooses to use them. Sadly, too many of our Brethren never come to the realization of their true purpose as a member of this beautiful fraternity."

"Right again, Brother Chris," he squealed in excitement as he got in his truck and leaned his head out the window. "That's exactly it. But I have another one that my Dad used to say all the time, and I am having trouble figuring out the lesson in that one. He used to say, 'You tell it the way you want to hear it, and I will feed it a bale of hay"

I just stared at him in silence as if John had just spoken in some foreign language. I wasn't even sure I had heard him right. Then, seeing the look on my face, he let out a big John laugh, threw the truck in gear, and said as he pulled out of the drive, "Think about that one…see you next month." My head is spinning again.

CENTER POINT STATION; THE REPRIEVE; AND REAL CHANGE

Sometimes your biggest pain-in-the-rear turns out to be your best angel. The truth is that I made a promise I shouldn't have made. Getting ready for Christmas this year has been pretty rough. Between Pam's work and mine, with the extra hours she had to put in this year, it was challenging to keep up with getting presents. Our family is scattered all around the Country. They are in Dallas, Houston, and even Lubbock. Also, we have relatives in some other States; Oregon, Oklahoma, and Arizona. So the end result is that we got everyone else's gifts taken care of except each other. Our promise to each other was that on the day after Christmas, I would take her anywhere she wanted to buy whatever she wanted. Therein lies the mistake, because she chose the outlet malls. Now I realize that most of the readers of this column, being men, may have never heard the phrase, *outlet malls,* but those of us who have, know that they are words that strike fear into the hearts of all husbands.

Simply defined, an outlet mall is a whole bunch of different stores all in one place where everything is on sale. I don't mean a bunch of stores like a regular mall either. To visit all of the stores in an outlet mall, one has to either walk the equivalent of ten miles by foot or continually move the car, so it's not more than a quarter of a mile from you at any one time. The latter being the most acceptable so that a regular depository for purchased items is pretty close at hand. The outlet mall is a wife's dream and a husband's nightmare, especially if he has made the mistake of promising to accompany her.

So there I was, bags in hand, following Pam as she happily went from one store to another, touching every item in every store, keeping the truck as close as possible to cut down on my personal mileage, when the phone rang. It is hard to visualize a 6ft 7 inch 275-pound redneck cowboy as an angel, but he was sure that right then. Big John was passing through and wanted to meet and eat (of course) and hopefully give me something for this month's article. As it turned out, he was headed our way down I-35, so after checking with Pam, who was ready for a break (thank God), we met across the highway at a place called the Center Point Station. I had never eaten there but had heard about how good it was. I didn't care how good it was; I just wanted to sit down for an hour or so.

It turned out to be a really neat little place. It was a country store and a restaurant both. Pam hadn't seen John for a while, and he had apparently eaten there before, so I let them chit-chat while I checked the menu. Now I have a weakness for a sandwich called a Patty Melt. Just like every other kind of food, there were all kinds of versions of the patty melt. This version looked pretty good in the picture. It had the meat, cheese, grilled onions as in most, but the bread was Texas toast, and it had bacon added. I just had to have one, and I ordered mine with fries and a big iced tea.

Pam ordered a regular cheeseburger and a drink. She moved aside so John could tell the guy at the register what he wanted. I grabbed Pam's drink cup to get her drink while she went to look for an empty table. I got the drinks and found Pam at a table for four (She's an intelligent lady who knows how much John eats) in the back. Pretty soon, John appeared, drink in hand, and he and Pam proceeded to exchange pictures of Grandchildren and stories of Christmas and family the day before. Within a couple of minutes, a young lady appeared with a big basket of fried pickles and some ranch sauce to dip them in. John must have ordered them, and I knew how he wasn't about to share; he didn't.

Pam likes fried pickles, and before I could stop her, she reached for one. I waited for the reaction from John that never came. He happily shared his pickles with her but gave me a quick warning look so I wouldn't even try to take one. He is supposed to be my Brother. Before long, our lunch arrived in the hands and arms of three servers, one for Pam's and mine and two for John's. The bottomless pit had ordered a patty melt like mine with fries, of course, and a cheeseburger and fries like Pam's. He had also gotten a chicken fried steak dinner complete with mashed potatoes and green beans and more gravy than he needed. I thought I saw a piece of pecan pie underneath one of his burger baskets. *Wow,* I thought. *Now Pam will see first-hand what I deal with having to buy John's lunch every month.*

I looked down at my patty melt and nearly fainted. It was two patties of meat instead of one large patty, and it had double cheese, a large number of grilled onions, six slices of bacon, and each slice of the Texas toast was at least an inch and a half thick. There was no way I was going to eat all of that and still walk. John saw my distress and grinned and said. "Just cut it in half and pass the other half over." I did that gladly, and we began to enjoy our lunch. I have to say that it was one of the best patty melts I have ever had. Pam seemed to like her burger, and of course, John was in hog heaven with the mountain of food he had ordered. While other diners stared and shook their heads, we ate in almost silence.

As I ate, I wondered if the message John had for the month would be something he was comfortable saying in front of Pam or if he even wanted to. Maybe I wouldn't even push him for something today. There was still a week before the end of the month. Perhaps we could get together again. My solitude and thoughts were cut short by a voice coming from somewhere behind the mound of debris across the table, which I recognized as Brothers John's, exclaiming, "Whoa.... whoa.... now that was a Hell of a meal." Right at that moment, a busboy appeared before us clothed in rubber gloves and an apron. He proceeded to clear away all non-edible items from the table.

Soon John appeared across the table, and without prompting, he just began to talk, "Brother Chris, I don't know what it is about that time between Christmas and the New Year that makes me think back not only on the previous year but on the many years before as well as the New Year coming up. You know that I don't believe in coincidences or even luck, for that matter. I know there is a plan for each of us; we have to take a broader look to see it. Well, there I was, the day before Christmas, wondering what I would talk to you about when we got together this month. I had a lot that was on my mind but nothing interesting enough to use. Then, when we were having our Christmas with the family on Christmas eve, my seven-year-old Granddaughter handed me a drawing that she had made for me for Christmas. She said it was a special picture just for me. Heck, it didn't matter to me what it was or what it looked like, Hailey had given it to me, and I loved it.

I looked down at the colored drawing on the paper and saw a picture of the moon. She drew a large moon in the middle of the paper and the sun in the left-hand upper corner, and in the upper right corner, she drew a dark quarter moon. The moon in the middle was lit up on three-quarters of its surface by the sun, while the remaining quarter was dark. Being a Mason and seeing the sun and the moon and what seems to be a depiction of a *from darkness to light* moment, I was eager to hear what she had to say about the drawing. Mind you, it was the evening of Christmas eve, and she had drawn it for me for Christmas just that day. Also, remember that this is a seven-year-old little girl who I believe is intelligent beyond her years even though I am her grandfather. When I asked her what it was, she said it was 'The Sun and the Moon together.' I asked what it meant, and she told me that she didn't know, but she just thought I would like it."

John shook his head slightly, looking off in the distance, and as I waited for him to continue his thoughts, I realized that the picture had flashed into his mind, and he was marveling over it again. "Brother Chris," he said, still visualizing that picture. "There is so much moral and Masonic symbolism in that picture. There are also life lessons in that picture. I sat there watching everyone open their gifts, thinking about the cost of some of them, and I looked down at the picture in my hands and realized that what I was holding was worth much, much more. Even with all the chaos that was going on around me, my mind was racing. That picture made me think about many things that were bothering many other people and me right now, in a slightly different way. It made me think about good versus evil and about right versus wrong. It made me think about something that is happening around us right now that will happen whether we like it or not. That thing is change. The world is changing, and there is no stopping it. And we will have to change with it. We have no choice. How we change is our decision, but you can be sure that change is going to happen."

"OK, John, I get it. Everything is changing, but how does that relate to Masonry and our Lodges? My newsletter is Masonic, after all."

John glanced over at Pam and said, "He is always butting in and getting sarcastic with me. It is distressing sometimes."

Before I could respond, Pam nodded in agreement, "He does that to me too. You just have to ignore it and go on."

John turned back to me, and the distressed look on my face gave me a cocky little smile and went right on. "Masonry and our Lodges have to change also. We will either change or we will die. It is ultimately our choice. Masonry, as a Fraternity, has always changed as society has changed. Those who believe that Masonry has remained the same throughout history as it has during their lifetimes need to do some serious study of history. Masonry is and has always been representative of the good in society. The job of Masons and Masonry is to be a force for good in this world and to influence others by the example we set. To accomplish our task, we must have a constant influx of new members. That means that to attract new members today, our Fraternity must be relevant to today's men.

Relevancy, in this case, comes in two parts. First, by its basic principles and its exclusive way of teaching those principles, Masonry will always be relevant to any man of any age at any time. But that is not enough by itself. Over and above the receiving of the lessons of Masonry, the Lodge must offer an atmosphere and chemistry that men of today desire. It must all fit into a package that is inclusive of the family. We have to accept that there will be change, and instead of wringing our hands and complaining, we need to guide that change and, in some cases, lead that change. We need to do that as Masons in our Lodges as well as citizens in our communities, State, and Country."

To my shock, Pam interrupted him to ask, "I like what you are saying, but how exactly do you intend to guide that change, John." She has always been a little skeptical that Masons could have any real effect on the whole of society.

Of course, instead of growling at her for interrupting, which wouldn't have been good for either of us, John smiled and said, "That's a good question, and I have an idea how, but it seems almost too simple. I think the way to guide change is to bring people out of darkness into the light. We need to educate them, or better yet, make them want to be educated. Then use that education to create an atmosphere of doing right, no matter what and to always do good instead of bad, eliminating evil wherever it exists instead of ignoring it and hoping it will go away."

John was talking only to her now, and I kept the recorder running as he continued, "Change is inevitable. The word change should be a good word and should be a good thing instead of the bad thing it has become over the last several years. We should not only embrace change but lead the change. Change that is borne of a true need, acknowledged by the majority, after a study of the facts, and after sufficient discussion, and then voted on by all who can and should vote is the bedrock of our Lodges. It is also the bedrock of our communities, our States, and our Country. Unfortunately, self-serving and sometimes hidden agendas pushed by groups who use a combination of untruths and half-truths to convince an uneducated and uncaring membership and populace to help them is the biggest threat to the future of our Lodges as well as the society around us. We don't realize that some have no care for the good of all. Their need for me clouds their perception of right and good.

This type of agenda pushes people down instead of helping them up. Ultimately those in need are tricked into believing they have no future. The end result of unconditional handouts and support is to discourage and ultimately deny self-sufficiency and the desire to do better. But I am heading off the main track here, but it is necessary to illustrate a point of self-sufficiency that when the thirteen colonies declared their independence from England, there were estimated that two-tenths of one percent of that population were Masons. A close study of history confirms that our

Masonic ancestors, living by and influencing those around them by their Masonic principles, led to the revolution and the formation of this Country and its government. Two-tenths of one percent of the population today would be approx. 750,000. It is estimated that there are 1.4 million Masons in the United States today, and that does not include the Prince Hall membership, which I believe should be counted as they abide by the same principles. Twice the percentage of Masons today than 230 years ago, and yet it can be argued that the influence of Freemasonry on the total population today is virtually non-existent.

In my opinion, the fault lies totally with us. Over the last two centuries, little by little, and aided by things like the Morgan Affair and the Anti Masonic movement, have caused our Fraternity to become more guarded in its actions. The result has been that Masons have withdrawn within the closed doors of their Lodges. Ultimately, the influence of Freemasonry upon the population of the United States has greatly disappeared. What was at one time the organization for good that almost all business and government leaders wanted and needed to be a part of has become unnecessary, unwanted, and unneeded for those men. I believe that this Country has suffered greatly because of this. There was a time when Masonry in this Country was very public and on display to everyone. The funeral of our Country's founder, George Washington, was a public celebration of his life and his Masonic membership. There were always parades in cities around the Country in which Masons marched clothed as Masons and were accepted and admired for their being a member of the Fraternity. Cornerstone ceremonies were much more public than those today. Freemasonry was woven deeply and publicly into the fabric of America. They preserved their secrecy and privacy simultaneously, and everyone knew that the Masons were good men dedicated to doing good and right. They were involved in their communities in many capacities, but their Masonic membership was common knowledge, and they were respected and admired for it.

Over the past eighty years, our wise leaders, thinking they were doing the right thing for Masonry, have pulled Masonry away from the public and done us much more harm than good. A Grand Orator a few years ago said that our goal should be: *'for all people to recognize and appreciate Freemasonry as an institution that exists for the benefit of mankind, without question.'* He is absolutely right, of course. But how can we possibly do this without getting out into the public? But there is still much fear within the Fraternity that the more people know about us, the worse it will be for Freemasonry. I say that's a load of bull. We worry that people will learn our private things, things in our ritual. I have two things to say about that. First, anyone who wants to know what goes on in our ritual only has to do a search on the internet or take a trip to the local book store to satisfy their curiosity. But what they never will realize is that just like a special meal made with a secret recipe, you may have all the ingredients out for all to see, but it is the finished product after all those ingredients have been put together in the perfect way that makes it special, and so it is with our Craft. The only way to know Freemasonry is to experience Freemasonry.

I know that you all need to get back to your shopping, so I will say this and then shut up. We must stay exclusive and only allow the right men into our ranks. We must understand that we are already an institution that exists for the benefit of humankind without question, but unless we show that we are to the world, they will never know. We must change the perception of our Fraternity to allow the public to know who we are. Let them see us as husbands and fathers and citizens of our communities, regular men, good men, who educate themselves and work to make themselves better. We must work for right and good, reject wrong and bad, and help destroy evil wherever it exists. We must come to a better understanding of what we are and what we are here to do. We must drag ourselves from the darkness that is now upon us into the light and make our Fraternity the influence upon humanity it was intended to be. We must do these things as a Fraternity and not just as individual Lodges.

As we endeavor to accomplish these things, good men will begin to flock to our Lodges to be a part of something as good and right, and as genuine as Freemasonry. Instead of fighting change, we will make change. We will guide change for the benefit and good of all."

With that, Big John Deacon stood up and announced that he needed to get back on the road, gave Pam a hug and a kiss, gripped my hand as a Master Mason and Brother, and disappeared out the door.

I was still mesmerized and thinking about all he said and wondering if I could put it all in the newsletter without making some Brothers mad. Pam's voice next to me cut short my daydream, "That was pretty good, and I am glad we got to see John, but we have shopping to do." With a groan, I realized that she was right and caught the attention of one of the servers to get our check which I was sure would come close to equaling the national debt. She informed me that everyone pays when they order, which meant that John had bought our lunches.

Wow, he continues to be a pain in my rear end because now Pam thinks that I just pay every time because I want to. Although, I'll bet he did this on purpose. Oh well, it is what it is. But I couldn't help thinking as we finished our walk around that mall that this whole pontification was the result of a picture drawn and given with love to a Grandfather by his

Granddaughter for Christmas. Inspiration sometimes comes from the most unlikely places.

JUST A BUNCH OF LEFTOVERS AND HOW IT REALLY FEELS

I knew I was taking a chance sending Big John Deacon a text when I did it. John is self admittedly an electronically challenged person. He is one of the few people I have ever been around who, if every cell phone, fax machine, and computer suddenly disappeared, John would be back on an equal level with most of the population and be a very happy man. I had kind of a goofy plan half thought out, I admit, but the half that was thought out sounded pretty good to me partly because it would save me a lot of money and somewhat because it would ingratiate me with Pam. But, of course, if John never saw my text and never responded, the whole plan would be a failure. So I texted him the coordinates anyway, and then I waited.

I figure that about now you are waiting for me to give you some explanation, so here it is. John had called a couple of days before and told me approximately when he would be in town and decide on a good place to eat. It was the day he was arriving, and I still hadn't decided on a place to eat. I walked into the kitchen and saw Pam was standing in front of the refrigerator, shaking her head. I heard her mutter something about throwing everything away and starting over. I looked over her shoulder and realized it was so jam-packed full of leftovers that there was no place to put anything else. There was no way to tell what was there because everything was inside a Styrofoam or plastic container. That's when the plan started taking shape. I went out to the garage and got the big Yeti cooler and told Pam that I would get rid of all the leftovers for her. She gave me a *you are crazy look,* shook her head, and walked away. With my Mom's voice in my mind telling me *not to waste food* because kids were starving in other countries, I crammed that cooler completely with every size and kind of container imaginable. I put a little ice on top and loaded it up into the truck, and waited for the time for us to meet. I knew that nothing would go bad inside that Yeti. It is my opinion that there has not been invented a food that John Deacon does not like. So whatever was inside that Yeti cooler should be something he would eat, I hoped. What I didn't think about was if I would like any of it. It was one of those details I failed to think through.

I texted John the coordinates of a little spot on one of my Lodge Brother's ranches north of San Antonio that I am quite partial to. If there was one thing John did know how to use (because he was on the road all the time) was his navigation device in the truck. The coordinates I gave him were to a little meadow surrounded by pretty old and large Oak trees. On one side of the field is a creek that flows year-round. On the opposite side is a sheer cliff rising a hundred feet up from the meadow base. Trees and rock formations, and all kinds of other vegetation cover the ridge. I don't think I have ever looked up at it and seen the same thing twice. The sound of the breeze rustling the leaves on the Live Oaks and the sound of the water flowing over the rocks in the creek are about the most relaxing sounds I have ever experienced. Even better was that right in the middle of that meadow was laid out complete with log benches and officers stations, which resembled a Masonic Lodge Room. I needed to clean it up for a degree that we had planned in a few weeks. It just so happened that John needing to see me on this day and me needing to do a little maintenance on our outdoor degree site, along with needing to do something with the leftovers, all came together in a plan to take care of all three at the same time.

To my surprise and satisfaction, John texted me back and agreed to meet where I suggested. (I love it when a plan comes together) I made sure

I got there in plenty of time to set up a little (although very strong) aluminum table and two oversize chairs. I had a couple of plates, some plastic ware on the table, and some condiments that I had grabbed at the last minute. I didn't know if they would be needed, but it seemed the right thing to do. I drove through Bill Millers, a gallon of tea to get rounded out for what I hoped would be a satisfactory (and cheap) lunch with John. I figured if everything in the cooler was good enough for Pam, the nieces, and the granddaughters to eat, it was certainly good enough for John and me, I hoped. With everything ready, I sat down to await the arrival of Big John, the Sultan of snacks, the Chieftain of chow, the Lion of Lunch, the.....well, you get the picture.

It wasn't long that I began to hear a faint sound that got closer and louder quickly. I looked up in time to see that big black truck roaring across the clearing toward me at a higher rate of speed than was prudent for that place. As I was just about to run for cover, he slid to a stop in a cloud of dust. Instead of getting out of the truck, he just sat there looking around. I waited for a couple of minutes and finally walked over to the driver's door and spread my arms apart like, "what the heck are you doing"?

I could see him still looking all around as he rolled his window down a fraction of an inch, "I must have ticked off a bunch of bees back up the road a ways, and they came after me. Are they gone?"

"John," I said, trying to keep the aggravation out of my voice. "Get out of the truck. There are no bees here." Then, as he slid down and followed me, still looking around, I muttered just loud enough for him to hear, "They probably know you have to come back by them on the way out and are waiting for you."

I heard him say, "*WHAT???*" .... I ignored him, but I know that got him thinking because he kept looking back down the road every few minutes. "Why in the devil did you make me come way out here in the middle of nowhere," he growled. "It's probably at least forty-five minutes to the nearest eating place from here."

"I needed to clean a little on our outdoor degree site, you were in town, and if you brought something for the February article, then this will all work out good, and surely there won't be any distractions," I replied. "And I brought the lunch out here."

I opened up the tailgate of my truck, sat the tea on the table with a couple of big cups, and proceeded to take all the containers one by one out of the cooler. When the last container was on the table, I handed John some utensils and told him to dig in.

"This looks like just a bunch of leftovers."

I laughed and replied, "It is leftovers, and I don't even know what's in each of those containers. It's a surprise" The moment of truth was at hand as John reached for, with a frown on his face, one of the larger containers. Inside, to my shock, it looked to me like a fully cooked T-bone steak. Then I remembered that we had grilled some steaks for a Sunday family get-together a couple of weeks before, and I forgot that we hadn't eaten all of them. John had hit the jackpot right off and reached for another container with some beans inside. John seemed to, at the moment, be enjoying this surprise lunch, so I reached for a container for myself. I opened the lid, and I would have bet my paycheck that what I was looking at could not be classified as belonging to any one of the four food groups.

I was not even sure it was meant to be eaten at all. Surely, it had come from a restaurant that one of my nieces had visited. John saw me staring apprehensively at the contents and reached across the table and took it. I could tell that he didn't know what it was either, but he sniffed it once, decided it wouldn't kill him, and took a taste. To this day, I still don't know what it was, but I do know that John liked it because he ate every bite of it. I reached for another container and got a large leftover helping of macaroni and cheese and another which had something that looked like chicken. It tasted like chicken, but it could have been anything because we all know that almost everything tastes like chicken. I saw John reach out for another big container. When he opened it, he made a face and slid it back. Curious about what food John would possibly reject, I opened it to take a look. I have no idea what it was, but it contained two different items, and it looked like one was eating the other. With John nodding his approval, it went right into the garbage bag I brought for our trash.

As John reached for another surprise, I asked him how he liked being out in the meadow. That got me a look of shock and confusion as he chewed. John swallowed and said, "What kind of crazy question is that, Brother Chris? This is what my Dad used to call the boondocks….as in out in the middle of nowhere."

"Well," I said, looking around. "This is one of my favorite boondocks, calm, relaxing, with the sounds of the trees and the water is like soft music playing." John rolled his eyes and grabbed another container, and happily found a couple of fried chicken legs. He took a bite out of one and grunted his approval as he sat back and looked around at the countryside while I talked. I didn't know if he had grunted his approval of the chicken legs or what I was talking about, so I kept on talking, "I come out here sometimes to sit, close my eyes, and think about stuff. It is so far out of the way that you don't have to worry about anyone or anything interrupting you." John nodded in agreement as he grabbed another container in which he found leftover pot roast complete with potatoes, carrots, and some gravy which I knew was tasty even cold. I sure wish I had grabbed that one, and he knew it by the look in my eyes as he smiled and took another big bite.

I realized that I hadn't eaten much and grabbed at one of the last containers left just as he did. I managed to slide it out from under his massive paw over to my side of the table. I cautiously peeked inside, and to my surprise, there were four leftover cheese enchiladas Pam had made a few days before. John herded the remaining three containers over to his side. As he opened each one, he smiled to his satisfaction and had them gone in no time. Finally, there being no more food available, John sat back to wait for me to finish eating.

As he sat there leaning back in his chair, he closed his eyes for a few seconds and began to see a change come over him. It was at first barely noticeable, but soon it was evident that something had changed. He gazed at the trees and then across to the bluff on the other side. He glanced over at our outdoor makeshift Lodge room and smiled. It was a smile to no one in particular but a reaction to what he was thinking. It was just John and his thoughts. I think he had forgotten I was there. I didn't know what John saw in his mind, but I carefully, without him knowing it, pushed the on switch on my recorder and waited, hoping he might put some of those thoughts into words. I didn't have to wait long. The breeze in the trees and the soothing sounds of the water had worked their magic and made John's thoughts turn into words, and those words just came flowing out. He had been looking at the makeshift Lodge room and just began talking.

"I remember the night I was made a Mason. A Brother told me beforehand that when I was done with my first initiation, I would go home that night a different man, the same, but different. I wondered how the heck he knew that, but I found out a couple of hours later that he was right. I was the same, but different. I went home that night, my big head and heart filled with something wonderful that I couldn't completely explain. I had to get a little older and wiser to figure it out."

I wanted to ask John what it was he figured out, but there was no way I was going to interrupt his thoughts. I was just glad I had thought to turn on the recorder.

I saw a smile form on his face as he continued, "I remember looking up into the face of my new Brother as he shined a new light into me. I was like a young child eager to receive any and all knowledge. That eagerness and desire to learn instilled in me that night has never gone away. Every time I have had the honor of being the one dispensing light, I have never forgotten how I felt that first night. How important it is to make sure that when I transform a good man from a Mister into a Brother. The experience lasts a lifetime, and his eagerness to receive light never goes away."

John was still looking at the outdoor Lodge, and it seemed like he was in some trance as he continued, "The night I was raised, it became clear to me that I could never go back to being my old self. There was no old self to go back to. Everything had changed, and every perception had changed. Every thought and action would now be judged and re-judged by myself using a Masonic filter for quality. Being satisfied by the status quo would never again be acceptable. The need to push for good, better, and for truth would always be there."

John paused for a few seconds. I thought he was done; as he continued to look at the outdoor Lodge room, I saw his eyes get a little misty as another memory, this a sad one, made its way into his consciousness. Big John swallowed heavily. I leaned in a little closer to hear him as he said just above a whisper, "Being more in tune with all people and their troubles in life, especially our Brothers and families, that being part of our teachings, has made me angry at times. Death and dealing with it was uncomfortable, but I learned a great lesson when one of my Brothers fought cancer.

I visited him right after a series of tests were done. The nurse had just wheeled his bed back into his room. He held out his hand to me, and I grasped it as he lay there. I looked into his eyes as he shook his head slightly to tell me that all hope was gone and that his time was almost over. As I stood there hurting inside for him, thinking how unfair it all was, he smiled. I could see that he wasn't afraid or angry at all and that he was ready to make this new journey, to take his place next to his creator. He was a Freemason who had learned his lessons well and knew that his greatest glory was ahead, not behind him. So at his memorial service, I couldn't help smiling, knowing that he was continuing his journey to the light."

John paused to take a breath, and something caught in my throat as I gasped. I don't know if it was emotion or, ... oh heck, who was I kidding. I know it was emotion, and I couldn't help it, but that sound had brought John out of his thoughts. I was mad at myself for causing it. He didn't seem to mind, though, because he just smiled, and lucky for me, he wasn't done yet.

"Brother Chris, I have been blessed to have been able to be a part of many Masonic ceremonies and honoring many worthy Brothers. I have looked into the eyes of a Brother who I was privileged to honor with a 60-

year service award from our Grand Lodge. As I spoke the mandated words of praise and thanks to each Brother for being a Mason for 60 plus years, I began to understand that giving the award was as fulfilling as receiving it. Looking into his shining eyes, there was a connection to him through Masonry that I could not have imagined. For those sitting on the sidelines watching, it was a great honor for the recipient. Still, they had no idea of the profound feeling of pride that awarding it to him gave me, and it made me more aware and gave me a greater understanding of the length and strength of what we Masons refer to as our mystic tie." John stopped talking all of a sudden and was gazing around him.

"Wow, John, you have really lived your Masonry."

"Brother Chris," he whispered. It's about more than just Masonry. Freemasonry is but a part of the whole. It's about knowing and understanding. It's about feeling and being aware of the presence. It's about taking control by letting go."

"Wait a minute," I exclaimed… suddenly seeing what was in front of me the whole time. "You are talking about Him, aren't you? You are talking about the Great Architect of the Universe. You have seen Him."

"Yes, my Brother," John said with a knowing smile. "I am talking about God. Yes, I have seen Him. I have talked to Him. And more importantly, He has talked to me."

"Tell me about Him; what does he look like," I asked anxiously?

John laughed and said, "It is not about what He looks like, it's about who He is and what He is. He is you, and He is me. He is this beautiful meadow, the trees, and the water. He is everywhere, and He is right here, right now. So when you let His presence and influence take you by the hand, the result is always good.

Thank you for bringing me out here, where it is so relaxing. It makes me begin to realize and understand things I hadn't before. God, the Great Architect, or whatever you or anyone wants to call Him, has given me many things. He has given me eyes to see what I could not before. He has taken away all fear. He has given me the strength to speak when I would not or could not before. He has given me all these things and much more. He stands ready to give to you and anyone all these things and more. It was no coincidence that your leftovers and this place came together with you and me today. No matter who you give credit to, it was something we both needed."

John was right, of course, and I told him so. I also told John that I had recorded the whole thing, and I would erase it if he wanted.

John laughed, "I saw your recorder sitting there and figured you were getting it all. I don't want what I said to ruffle any feathers, but it's not very logical that people think God is only found in church or a Holy Book. He is everywhere and in everything, and I sometimes see Him in my mind's eye, looking around at what we have done with Him and to Him, and because of Him. I know He's not happy with all of it. If you want to use it, I am ok with it. I am not ashamed of it."

With that, John got up and headed to his truck. I grabbed something out of my truck and followed him. As John swung his big frame up into his truck, I handed him two slices of pecan pie that I bought when I bought the tea at Bill Millers. That made his day as he hauled his rotund rear end out of the truck to give me a big John Deacon bear hug. Then he was gone in a cloud of dust. I was in no hurry and sat down to enjoy my pie and in the quiet and stillness of that beautiful place broken only by the rustle of leaves and the soothing sound of water lightly slapping the rocks.

I swear I could feel it...I could feel Him.............

CROSSROADS
Saloon & Steakhouse

THE CROSSROADS AND MASONRY IS TOLERANT OF ALL RELIGIONS

It had been a pretty relaxing day overall. Almost everything had gone pretty well, and there had been nothing more stressful than that aggravation you feel when eating lunch in your car and reaching for a few fries, and as you bring them toward your mouth, one manages to fall. Watching, mesmerized as if in slow motion, it falls and bounces off your leg, then over against the center console, bouncing back towards you, landing on the edge of the seat, teetering on edge for what seems like forever before slipping down into that abyss, that black hole, between the console and the seat, from which no fry ever returns. Yup, it had just happened to me.

As I sat there contemplating how bad I wanted that particular fry and wondering if I could retrieve it. I realized that there was more down there and the real possibility that I could latch on to a very old and a very hard French fry; my phone rang and thankfully interrupted any further thoughts of attempting a rescue. When I answered, I heard an out of breath John Deacon.

"Brother Chris, meet me in Fredericksburg at the Crossroads Steakhouse after work for dinner. I have a big meeting with some construction people in the morning; then I have to head home. I won't be coming all the way down to you. I have something really important to tell you."

I decided to have some fun with him. "So you are not asking me to dinner; you are ordering me to dinner? I don't think that is right" That confused him a little and then aggravated him.

"What the heck are you talking about? Are you jerking my chain? Maybe I should take you outside when you get here and teach you some manners."

"Except that it wouldn't be a fair fight," I replied.

"Why not," John shot back?

"Because," I said slowly for effect. "I would be outnumbered two to one."

John paused for a few seconds before he replied, "I suppose that is a reference to my size."

"You would suppose right," I answered, glad that he couldn't see the grin on my face.

"I can't believe you would talk that way to a Brother," he offered, sounding a little hurt.

"I can't believe a Brother would offer to whoop my rear end," I shot back.

"Hmmm," he said. "Touché, my Brother, touché. Where was I? Oh yes," John went right on. "So, can you be up here or not?" There was no point in giving John another hard time, so I told him I would be there.

Two things made me agree to have dinner with him, ok, three. The first was that it was only an hour away. Second, Pam was out of town on business, so I would have been eating alone anyway. Oh, and third, I had eaten at the Crossroads before, and it was excellent. They have an appetizer, jalapenos stuffed with BBQ brisket and wrapped in bacon. They serve them on a bed of grilled onions with a smoky BBQ dipping sauce. I thought about it all the way up there with my mouth-watering.

It was just after dark when I pulled into a parking slot in front of the restaurant. About six spaces away, I could barely make out the outline of a big black F350, aka *Blackie*. It was empty; I didn't figure he would be able to wait for me anyway. This restaurant is a steakhouse with a bar attached. The bar has a stage and a dance floor and has an 1800s look and feel. They also have a little room with four tables in one corner down one flight of stairs that I think used to be a wine cellar. It is secluded down there. That's where I found Big John alone and secluded out of sight, out of mind, out of the way.

He was concentrating on the plate of brisket stuffed jalapenos in front of him. Then, finally, he looked up and saw me and waved me down the stairs. I sat down opposite him. Our server, Lynn, who must have followed me down the stairs, asked what I wanted to drink. Since it was after work, I ordered my favorite adult beverage and a plate of those brisket jalapenos. John ordered himself another round of the same. Finally, I settled back in my chair and asked John how his week was going. Instead of the usual "everything is fine," he proceeded to unload on me.

"Brother Chris, I have had a very traumatic week." I thought about telling him about my French fry issue, so he wouldn't think he was the only one with problems, but decided not to.

"What happened, John?" I asked sympathetically.

"I've been on the road all week," John said, shaking his head. "Yesterday, I drove through a fast-food restaurant to get something for lunch, and I parked next to a business that had a go-kart track next to it. As

I was sitting there in my truck having my lunch, enjoying the cool air conditioning, I started hearing a moan which sounded like it was coming from under the hood of my truck. And as I sat there trying to figure out where it was coming from, it kept getting louder and louder and louder until I thought the engine was going to explode. I kept checking the gauges to see if something was wrong, but they never showed anything. No warning lights came on either, and I was looking around at other people to see if they heard it, and no one seemed to have heard it. Finally, I thought I was going crazy. In a panic, I jumped out of the truck and ran about 10 yards away from it. It was then that I realized that the sound was not coming from my truck, but it was coming from behind me. When I turned around, there was a guy with a very loud leaf blower blowing the debris off of the go-kart track. I must not have been the only dumb hombre to have ever fallen for that because he just laughed at me as I walked back to my truck."

I have to tell you, dear Reader, that I could not help it. The look on John's face telling me about the noise, and the mental picture of his portliness bailing out of his truck, hamburger in one hand and a drink in the other (heaven forbid he should leave anything edible behind) was too much for me. I laughed long and hard while he just sat there and glared at me.

"*It's not THAT funny!*" John finally growled. "You should be glad that it didn't blow up and that I survived. Otherwise, where would your column be without me?"

Before I could respond with the proper sarcasm, Lynn appeared with my drink and our appetizers. She was ready for us to order our entrées. I went first and ordered Chicken Fried Steak with asparagus and mashed potatoes for my sides. John proceeded to match my order and added a T-Bone steak, a New York strip with broccoli, sautéed squash, two baked potatoes, and some of their excellent sourdough bread. Lynn reviewed the three pages she filled up, gave John a quick wink, and left to turn in our order.

I could tell that John had something on his mind as we attacked our jalapenos. It is his history that it translates into a pretty good article when he is worked up about something. So, I asked him what was bothering him. He gave me a steady stare for several seconds before speaking, and when he did, it was in a low voice as if he was uncomfortable saying it, "Brother Chris, I am distraught….I am worried about our future."

"If you are talking about the future of Masonry," I replied. "Then so am I, John. I think we all are."

John acted like he hadn't heard me and continued, "I have traveled around this State and met a lot of Brothers. I have visited a lot of Lodges and seen a lot of Masonry. But, unfortunately, I have seen a lot of Masonry done wrong."

"What do you mean done wrong?"

"Well, when I get done telling you what's worrying me, you might not want to print it," he said slowly.

"Well," I said, smiling at my wit. "Spill it then, and we will see. Tell you what, If I can't or won't print it, then you have to buy lunch."

Just then, Lynn appeared with a mountain of food and began trying to find a place on our table for all of it. I was rather glad she showed up when she did because the look I got from John didn't quite say what I hoped it would say. Heck, who was I kidding? He was going to find a way to stick me with the bill anyway. This was one of the times I was glad that he lapsed into total silence and concentration as he ate.

My steak was delicious as always, and the only time John looked up from one of his plates was to make sure I was not infringing on any of his food. It took a while, but he finally got to the end. John is kind of like my old hound dog. When all the food is gone, she rechecks every possible nook and cranny to ensure nothing has been overlooked. That's John. I knew there was nothing left to find, but I waited patiently while he made sure.

When he was finally done, he looked up at me, leaned back in his chair, and took a deep breath. "Do you want to know what I heard in a Lodge last week?" he asked with a slight edge to his voice. I just sat and waited.

"I was in a Lodge, and the Chaplain said a prayer before our meal. He finished by dedicating his prayer in the name of the God of his specific religion."

"I had heard that done before too once, and the Brother had good council whispered in his ear shortly after. But, Yup, that's not right, John," I replied.

"Yer darn tootin' it's not right," John growled. "As I heard it, I realized something that scared the hell out of me. I wondered if the Brother who gave the blessing didn't know any better or that he did it on purpose. I wasn't quite sure at that point. But all the Brothers in the Lodge were definitely in agreement with him. And that fact told me that these men were not Masons. Oh, they all had dues cards that said they were. And they had keys to a Masonic Lodge, and I am sure they were all listed on the Grand Lodge membership database, but I was positive they weren't Masons."

My head was starting to hurt a little as I heard those last words. "John," I whispered, looking around to see if anyone heard him but only seeing four walls because we were down in a hole; I continued. "I am a little confused. I don't quite understand what you are saying."

"My Brother Chris," John said sternly. "Masonry holds sacred that a man has to have a belief in God as a basic qualification to being a Mason. It dictates that every Brother may believe as he desires and that his belief will never be considered better or worse than any other Brothers'. A Mason's religion is private to him. And not bringing up within the Lodge, discussing specific religion, including making what is supposed to be a non-partisan prayer partisan, is not practicing Masonry. Anyone who does not practice Masonry is technically NOT a Mason. It is that simple. There is no wiggle room here. It is a cornerstone of Freemasonry.

Any man who has passed through the forms and ceremonies of our initiations cannot possibly blame ignorance for violating this principle. That Brother has, for whatever reason, totally missed the whole point of Masonry. Speaking about missing the entire point, I have seen ritual done in my travels that bears little or no resemblance to what is mandated by our Grand Lodge. When confronted about it, these Brothers will invariably answer that 'that's the way we do it out here,' or they smile and say that 'we do it our way here at the Grand Lodge of .... '(whatever name of their Lodge or area). These are the same Brothers who complain that the Grand Lodge never comes out to visit them or the Grand Lodge doesn't care about them. What they fail to realize is that the Grand Lodge is them. The laws and regulations of the Grand Lodge are made by a majority vote of the past masters and sitting masters of all Texas Lodges. Every Texas Lodge and every Texas Mason has the same laws and regulations to abide by."

"But John," I said, softly cringing a little. "To say that they are not Masons is a little harsh, isn't it?"

"What would you call it, Brother Chris?" John asked, spreading his hands apart. "A Masonic Lodge whose Brothers are pushing their specific religion in Lodge, regardless if every Brother in the Lodge belongs to the same religion or church, it's not Masonic. A Lodge whose Brothers give a watered-down, and in many cases, a barely recognizable version of the degrees and the words accompanying them or who will not learn how to open and close a Lodge properly is not practicing Masonry.

I don't know about you in your big city Lodges Brother Chris, but my Lodge is out in the country, and they are always wondering why the movers and shakers in their communities aren't Masons anymore. One of our charges states that being a Mason and following its principles will *distinguish us from the rest of the community and mark our consequence among Masons.'*

Whenever men research Masonry before visiting a Lodge for the first time, they find that it is an organization that provides things they are missing in their own lives, things they desire, and men they wish to be associated with. They are looking for honesty, integrity, professionalism, and they are looking for structure and discipline. When they see that Masonry provides all of these things in their research, they want to be a part of it. But when they go to the Lodge, they often find things are much different from what they supposed. Why would any man, much less a mayor, a councilperson, banker, or businessman, want to belong to an organization that doesn't follow its foundations and precepts?

When someone sees a Mason, they should immediately know that he is honest, professional, and disciplined, a man of integrity. By possessing these qualities, he should be easily identifiable as a member of the Fraternity. Where a Mason should stand out from the crowd as an upright person, most of us are indistinguishable from the rest of the public. Our job is to change society by setting an example of exemplary behavior. It does not mean that we should blend in and not cause trouble. A Brother who seeks to set an example by blending in has missed an essential lesson in Masonry."

"I see what you mean now, John," I told him cautiously. "I just never heard anyone tell a Brother who had gone through the degrees that he was not a Mason." John nodded his head sadly, got a pained look on his face, and I watched him change from angry and agitated to thoughtful and sad.

"I am sorry, my Brother," John said, still shaking his head. "But it's the way I see it. Any organization is only as good as its members. And I am sorry to say that we have some members who have had little or no education, others who have chosen not to learn, and others who sadly don't care and don't believe in Masonry."

"So, how are you going to fix it, John? You can't complain about a problem unless you have a solution."

"Well, I do have a couple of ideas. I think that I agree with you that a lot more education is needed. I think you need to get that education committee you belong to off of their educated rear ends and get out there and teach more Masons."

"But John," I interrupted, knowing he was not going to like it. "We do at least five Officer Leadership Training Programs a year We cover most of the State. But there are only a certain number of Brothers who will show up."

"Well, then you need to invite and train trainers to pass the information to all the Brothers in all the Districts in the State." That was a good idea, I thought, and I told him so as he continued.

"Secondly, our Grand Master, in his message to the Lodges passed through his District Deputies, has exhorted us all to *'plant the seed of Freemasonry'* to help members. In my opinion, I believe that the best way to plant the seed is to be what the Worshipful Master of one of my Lodges asked us all to be, and that is to be genuine Masons. We need to be the men that Masonry expects us to be and to always practice genuine Masonry."

John got up suddenly and said he had to go to the restroom. I thought I saw a bit of moisture in the corner of one of his eyes but dismissed it, figuring it was just one of his ways of getting out of paying the bill. I sure had a lot to think about, and I planned on doing it on the drive back home. I paid the bill, feeling sad I didn't get to say goodbye. John made some excellent points. I was almost out of town when my phone rang. It was John. I answered a little confused, and John immediately demanded to know why I left without saying goodbye. He scoffed at my suggestion that he was trying to get out of paying the bill.

John thanked me for dinner, believing in what he said, and passing along his words in our newsletter. I told him it was my honor, and at the same time, I thought, *It's a good thing you've got something to say, big guy, so I don't have to make it up.*

Then John hung up, and it occurred to me that it was probably a little tear I saw in the corner of his eye. He indeed is an old softy.

THE PROFOUND WORDS OF A MASON'S WIFE

I always get a little stressed towards the end of the month when I haven't heard from John. I rarely talk to him throughout the month because we are both so busy, and I know that sometime during that last week of the month, I will look up and see him driving into the shop, or I pick up the phone, and he will be there.

The month was two days from being over, and I hadn't heard a peep from John. Stress was not the descriptive word at this point. It was more like terror. I have long worried that the day was going to come when John might be sick or the victim of some other calamity that would keep him from enlightening me and the rest of the Masonic Fraternity about what was on his mind and in his stomach for that month. He was not answering his cell phone, and neither he nor Mrs. Deacon was answering their home phone. My first impression was that something had happened to him, and I know that if something did that, I wouldn't be too high on the list of those who got notified first. I have to admit to some uneasiness as he has been usually very faithful and punctual to his responsibility to support the newsletter. John could also be on a short vacation and forgot to tell me, or more likely, he just plain forgot about me and the newsletter. If he did, when I hear from him, I will say something about his having early Alzheimer's.

Unbelievably it was looking more and more like I would have to either make something up on my own or try to reuse an old John Deacon article. I wasn't too excited about either choice. As is my nature, I resolved to wait until the last possible minute to hear from him. By the time the last day of the month rolled around, and I still hadn't heard from him, I began to stress even more while racking my brain for something to put in the newsletter. Then out of nowhere, an email showed up in my spam box as I went there to delete all the usual garbage that shows up. There, right in the middle of a lot of scams and too good to be true offers, my eyes focused on one lone email. The reason it stood out was that it simply said, "Hello Chris" under the title. As I read that email, I couldn't help but think about my other Brother, Big John Deacon, who is fond of saying that there is no such thing as luck or coincidence. Things happen for a reason, and that if you step back and take a broader view of things, sometimes you see and understand more than before. The fact that I just happened to see that one email reinforces all that John has been saying. I knew as I read it that I needed to tell the story of how I received this particular email.

A few weeks ago, I was invited to speak at a Lodge to a group of Masons and their wives and a few non-Masons. Before the program, I talked to a newly initiated Entered Apprentice (and because we aren't allowed to publish names of EA's, I will call him John). So John and I were standing in the back of the kitchen before dinner was served. I asked him how he was progressing in his work and if he was happy that he had decided to be made a Mason. The EA told me that everything was moving well, and then he told me something that I believe all of us, or at least most of us, had experienced when we first made a Mason.

He told me that the night he was initiated as an Entered Apprentice, the experience made him happy and excited. Although he didn't quite understand it all yet, nor could he thoroughly explain it, he realized that he had just experienced something extraordinary. It was so overwhelming that deep down, he wanted to share it with someone. Moreover, he wanted to share this wonderful feeling with the one person he cared for most in his life……. his wife.

But there was one problem, and it wasn't until he was home and face to face with her that the realization hit him, that as bad as he wanted to share this happy occasion, he could only communicate to a point. They had told him to "keep the secrets,"……and although he wasn't quite sure specifically what those secrets were, he knew that he must not share them. As he told me about the mixed emotions of that face-to-face moment, I could hear the concern and a little confusion in his voice. I had heard it many times before and had many years ago felt the same emotions. He was thrilled and proud to be a Mason and looking forward to the journey before him with anticipation and excitement. But he was concerned about how she felt about it. He wanted and needed her continued blessings on his decision to join the Fraternity, but he knew that he could not correctly explain and share what he could, which bothered him.

I told him about the articles that John Deacon had shared with me late last year, and I told him I would send them to him with the hope that his wife might read them and gain a better understanding of not only what he had gone through but also why he was as concerned as he was. He thanked me for suggesting the two articles and assured me that he would gladly pass them to his wife to read.

The dinner and the program were perfect, and somewhere during the evening, I got to meet EA John's lovely wife (and keeping with certain anonymity, we will call her Kellie). She was gracious and seemed genuinely happy that John was a part of our great Fraternity. However, I wondered if underneath she might not be as happy as she sounded, and I hoped that the two John Deacon articles might help if she weren't. I thought about her and John a couple of times on the drive back the next day. I located the two past newsletters that I had told John about and sent them off to the Worshipful Master of the Lodge because I had failed to get John's email address. About a week later....in my spam as mentioned earlier box, I received the following:

Hello Chris,

I am Brother John's wife and was forwarded your September & October 2015 newsletters for the Davy Crockett Lodge #1225 by Brother Travis. I first and foremost want to say, Thank You for not only sending those letters to my attention but also for thinking that I would benefit from reading them. I thoroughly enjoyed every word written and the meaning behind each one of them. I am, as you know, a wife of a new Mason still going through his initial degree training, and this is all fairly new to me. I am very proud of my husband of almost 16 years, and I feel that since we were not able to conceive any children of our own, John has always searched for a greater "reason" for his life - and incomes Freemasonry. His love for God and his honest heart are what make me the proudest to be his wife - we are each a half, and together we make a whole. I find truth in your newsletter that with knowledge and clarity comes harmony and happiness - we live that each day as we seek God's truth in our daily lives. I know there will be things, times, words, tears, gestures, and struggles that John will not be able to share with me, but at the same time, I hope he will know that my hand and heart are on the apron strings he ties at each Lodge meeting. Will this be something new we have to find common ground in understanding? Yes, but that doesn't worry me? Will this be a commitment that sometimes might take him away from our home? Yes, but that doesn't worry me? I am proud, supportive, accepting, and pushing John to give this only life we're given, all he's got! I am and will forever be grateful to Freemasonry for giving my dear husband a reason to be a Better Man. God Bless You, Chris, and keep the newsletters coming!! Hope to see you again soon.

So, go ahead and reread it. Because I know you want to. I surely did. I am not too proud to say that I had to get up from my desk at work and take a trip to the restroom to retrieve some paper towels to wipe my eyes. After reading that heartfelt message from a loving and supportive wife talking about her husband, they had become blurry with excessive liquid buildup.

I will indeed have to tell her that they were the words of my friend and Brother, John Deacon, that had touched her. They inspired her to write such a touching tribute to her husband, our new Brother, and also to Masonry. I am just proud that I had a small part in it. It is always exciting to watch a new Mason just beginning his lifelong Masonic journey. So, as our new Brother Entered Apprentice sets out upon that path of Masonic Light, I can only say, "Enjoy, my Brother.... enjoy!"

As of the writing of this article, I still haven't heard from John. So if any of y'all out there see him or have any information as to his whereabouts, please let me know.

BILLY GENE'S

FINDING UNEXPECTED LIGHT AT BILLY GENE'S

Well, I finally found John, not that anyone was as worried about it as I was. As it turns out, he and Mrs. Deacon were having a happy, much deserved weeks' vacation on a cruise to the Caribbean. When he finally returned one of the many messages I left him, John tried to tell me that he had called and left me a message that they would be gone. I assured him that, had he left me a message, it was a good bet that I would not have been calling him and leaving him messages wondering where he was. Unbelievably, John saw the logic in what I said.

John called to tell me that he was in Kerrville for the day and would not have enough time to drive the 45 minutes to have lunch with me. I sure didn't have anything for this month's newsletter, so lunch in the big city of Kerrville sounded pretty good. On the way out the door, I hit up Uncle Google where we could get a good Chicken Fried Steak in Kerrville, and the name Billy Gene's Restaurant flashed up on the screen.

Precisely 35 minutes later, I pulled into Billy Gene's parking lot (I admit I did exceed the speed limit slightly on the way). From my parking place, I had a great view of the Guadalupe River, which was about 200 yards wide at this point. On the opposite side was a grassy rolling hill that seemed to go on forever. My moment of visual relaxation was interrupted by a large black F-350 parked in the one parking place that blocked my line of sight to the river. I looked at the driver expecting to see a huge cowboy grinning from ear to ear. Instead, I saw a really big cowboy with a serious look on his face. We crawled out of our trucks and walked side by side to the restaurant's door, and other than a handshake, no words passed between us. The usual jovial John was still on vacation, I guess.

The booth they sat us in provided a great view of the river. John was gazing at it and the hills behind it when I asked about his vacation on the ship. John's growling answer was, "I don't even like boats, I don't like surprises, and I don't know why the heck she surprised me with a trip on a boat." I started to tell him that it was a ship and not a boat, but I figured that would further aggravate him.

I asked him if he was ok. John got a sad look on his face and continued to look out at the river. I thought maybe he was irritated at me, but I hadn't done anything yet that I could think of to make him that way. I tried to talk to him a couple more times while we were looking at the menus, but all I could get out of him was, "Things aren't always what they seem to be, and people aren't always who you thought they were."

I was beginning to think I had made a mistake by meeting him when Kasey, our server, appeared to take our drink order. We ordered a couple of iced teas, and I noticed as she walked away that it looked like John was staring at her, specifically her right arm. I admit that she was very pleasing to the eye, but John was a married man. Now, I subscribe to the premise that if the Great Architect had not wanted men to look at women, he would have made them all look the same, but John was an older man, and she was less than half his age! John caught me looking at him funny-like and realized why and got real defensive. I could see a little red had started creeping up his neck.

"Cut that out," John growled at me. "I was looking at the tattoo on her arm. It was some writing that I couldn't quite make out." I was still looking at him funny and shaking my head when she returned with our drinks. What does that tattoo on your arm say?" John asked quickly, glancing sideways at me.

Her smile was quick and easy as she pulled up her sleeve and recited it to John. She said that when she read the words the first time they spoke to her personally, she had them put on her arm so she could always see them. After that, she said they held a special meaning to her. The words that circled her arm were, "Happiness can be found even in the darkest of times if one only remembers to turn on the light."

Imagine two old Masons sitting in a booth getting ready to have lunch, one bummed out for some reason. The other is waiting for some Masonic profundity from the other. Then, out of nowhere, almost as if it were written to happen that way, we would be there on that day at that hour with Kasey as our server, and that she would deliver 19 words that would leave us speechless and staring at each other. I can't speak for John, but it was one of those *aha* moments for me. As I sat there staring at John with all kinds of things running through my brain, I could vaguely hear Kasey telling John that she was a big Harry Potter fan. She read all the books, saw all the movies, and those words were spoken by one of the characters in the Potter books; the one and only Albus Dumbledore.

She had to ask us several times if we were ready to order before we snapped out of our trance. I had never laid the menu down. As I looked at it, my mouth immediately began to water. There was a lot of good stuff there, and I was sure that John would have at least one of everything. As I sat there in shock, I heard John order two Chicken Fried Steaks, a Pepper Steak, and a plate of Liver and Onions. A couple of the plates had mashed potatoes and gravy and green beans, another had a baked potato and okra, and the last had grilled veggies and French fries. Just listening to John's order made me feel full already. Somewhere along the line, a completely dumbfounded Kasey had stopped writing and, realizing it, had to catch up. She looked over at me, and I got the feeling that she half expected me to pass on lunch, but I quickly ordered Chicken Fried Steak, and off she went to turn in our order, still in disbelief. I think mentally calculating how many to-go containers she was going to need. Little did she know that there would be no leftovers ….in fact, when John got done, there would be little effort to expend in cleaning the dishes.

It wasn't long before Kasey returned with a small army of helpers carrying several trays piled high with food. The booth wasn't a huge one, so by the time all the plates were laid out on the table, my one plate was surrounded by several of John's. And true to his nature, he gave me the *evil eye* the whole time I was eating my lunch, making sure I didn't eat any of his. I thought about telling him, since he was probably going to find some way of sticking me with the bill, legally, all the food belonged to me, so anything I ate would be mine anyway. But since he was in a foul mood already, I didn't. It was a good thought, though.

John dug right in like he hadn't eaten in a week, and I could tell he liked it. As for my Chicken Fried Steak, it was great. I have found that there are Chicken Fried Steaks that are better than others, and then a few are in a class all by themselves. I know that it's a matter of personal taste, but for me, this one was one of those in that special class. It was made the way I like it, the way my Mom used to make it. Apparently, John agreed because all I could hear from him was a constant stream of tasty yummy noises, which bordered on annoying. I ate slowly, enjoying every bite while John seemed to be afraid I would abscond with a bite off one of his many plates and was eating at a record pace even for him. I still got done about 20 minutes ahead of him. As usual, there was no conversation while he ate.

John was pretty religious about that rule. As I waited patiently for him to finish, I hoped that he had something worth sharing with me for next month's article.

He finished finally and turned to stare out the window at the river's peaceful flowing, and I began to think that he had nothing. Why the heck, then, did he make me come all the way out here to watch him eat and pay for it. So I waited until I couldn't stand it anymore, "John, I know you are upset, and I don't want to aggravate the situation, but I am not getting any younger over here. Do you want to talk about what's bothering you?"

Slowly he turned his head towards me and said, "No, there is no fixing some things. I was going to talk to you about something else, but since Kasey shared her tattoo with us, it has got me to thinking about something entirely different."

"Well, turn that thinking into words," I said quickly. "Because as much as I would like to, I don't have all day to spend sitting here with you" As usual, John ignored me; at least he acted like he did.

"You and I have talked a lot about Masonic Education," John said slowly, "and I think that we agree how important it is. Masons talk about *receiving light and instruction* and agree on darkness to light."

"I don't think most brothers realize that these are two different things." Man, I hated to interrupt because I know John hates it, but that statement caught me off guard.

"Whoa, up there, my Brother. I have never heard anyone say that..." I stopped John mid-sentence, and now he clenched his jaw and gave me the evil eye again, so I shut up. "Well, it's not hard to figure out that receiving light and instruction is about learning about Freemasonry, but *being brought from darkness to light* is about something more personal and more private. Before you ask, this is my opinion. Going through the degrees and learning the proper work is receiving light. Possessing the necessary working tools is receiving light. Learning all you can through study and participation, and meditation is receiving light. But *being brought from darkness to light* is different, and the Brother himself is the only one who knows when he has truly *been brought from darkness to light.*"

John paused to take a drink from his iced tea, and I took advantage of that pause to jump in and ask as nicely as I could, "What the heck are you talking about, John?" I quickly realized that it came out a whole lot louder and more forceful than I had intended, but I was confused! John swallowed and just stared at me for several seconds like he was trying to force some measure of understanding into my head mentally, or maybe he thought I was not as worthy and well qualified as he thought I was.

"Brother Chris," John finally said with a note of exasperation in his voice. "I believe that coming from darkness to light signifies an advanced state of enlightenment, and only you will know when and if you attain it. Masonry's ultimate purpose, which most every Mason fails to see or understand, is to truly know and understand his inner nature. Only then can he become the enlightened man he really wants to be."

I admit that I was starting to get a very faint glimmer of what he was talking about, but I was far from where I needed to be yet. Seeing this, he continued talking really slow (like that would make me understand better).

"When we are born, at that moment, we are pure and innocent in every way. We have no prejudices, no anger, no fears, and no bad habits. Then almost immediately, we begin to acquire all of those things. But even as these things pile up, inside, our deepest desire is to get back to being that pure and innocent person as we were when we were born. Many don't realize this, and frankly, most are never able to realize it. Masonry is a science that allows a man to discover his deepest flaws and face who he is or who he has become. It teaches him to face those prejudices and anger and fears and allows him to begin to *divest his mind and conscience* of them in his quest to return to purity and innocence.

For several reasons, very few realize this path exists, and even fewer take up those Masonic lessons and those working tools provided and set out on what many Masonic scholars describe as a path to perfection. Although we know that true perfection is probably unattainable, the struggle of trying and the reward it brings are the true secrets we are searching for.... that which was lost. Those personal discoveries and sublime truths a man makes of himself, within himself, are the true secrets of Freemasonry. Those secrets are so unique, so private, and so important that a man will never reveal them to another, and even if he wanted to tell them, he couldn't possibly find the words to make them understood."

Then there was silence. John began to gaze out the window again at the river as I sat there staring into space. John's words were sinking into me. I had no trouble understanding his words or comprehending their meaning at all. The way he had said it was easy to follow. But it was the depth of what he had said that left me speechless. I was going to be thinking about this for a long time.

But I had a question. "John, you said that for several reasons, most Masons don't even know this path exists. What do you mean by that, and what are the reasons?"

Slowly his head turned back to me and he replied, "Yes, there are several reasons why Masons don't know that there is a path to a greater awareness of inner self. The first reason is that many do not believe there is anything more to Masonry than our basic rituals and lessons and, therefore, no reason to search. Another reason is that very few Lodges or Masonic organizations even attempt to teach Brothers beyond their Degrees and Catechism. Therefore, there is no stimulation of the intellect to ask questions and search for deeper meanings, leading to the discussion path. Another is that some men and Brothers understand and believe that what we call the secrets of Freemasonry, those secrets that anti-Masons are chasing, are but an outer veil that is meant to occupy those who are *not duly and truly prepared* and surely those who are *not worthy and well qualified.* I guess another reason is the perception that it is just too difficult. There is no doubt that it is hard, and to travel that path, you must want it badly.... very badly."

As I digested what John said, I saw Kasey slide the bill onto the table out of my peripheral vision. John reached for it. That brought me out of my spell and into reality. I looked up with a shocked look, thinking he was going to treat, which out of my peripheral vision, quickly turned to a frown as he gave it back to Kasey and ordered dessert.

"Is there no end to your appetite John," I asked, shaking my head?

"Brother Chris," Whether I am driving across the State, selling those working tools, or just sitting here talking to you, it works up my appetite. And I just saw they have pecan cobbler."

Well, at least he had the presence of mind to order dessert for me too. Kasey sure knew how to make two old guys smile cause when she sat our cobbler down in front of us; I saw that she had put a scoop of ice cream on top of each. Ohhh boy, that ice cream on top of that hot cobbler was sure good. But, unlike John, I ate it slowly and savored every bite. By the time I was done, John had lapsed into silence once again, and our bill had magically reappeared. I looked at the time and realized that I needed to get back.

"Is there anything I can do for you, John?" I asked.

He gave me a small smile as he slid out of the booth and said, "I am ok."

As I was paying the bill, John waved Kasey over and thanked her for sharing the message of her tattoo, and she gave him a big smile and hug. Then she was off to help her other customers. As usual, the big guy got the hug, but I guess he needed it. Walking out to the parking lot, I shook his big paw and thanked him for an enlightening lunch. That made John laugh out loud as I watched that big F-350 roar off down the road in a cloud of smoke.

As I drove along back to work, I was deep in thought. I'll bet you think I was thinking about the profound words of my Brother John, but no, I was thinking, *why does John get all the hugs from the ladies?*

WACO, VITEKS, AND MR. GUNSMOKE

Right at the moment, I was a little worried about Brad. Not that he was in any grave danger, but he was sitting next to the one and only Big John Deacon in the front of his big F-350 that he, way too affectionately, calls "Blackie".

So why was Brad riding with John, you ask? Well, it's like this for the first time since I can remember; the Grand Master had called a special Grand Lodge Communication to vote on only one piece of business. Apparently, when we voted in December to change the Annual Grand Communication to a different date, none of the 3000 or so Masons there realized that the date we picked was not going to work. I am not dogging any of my Brothers because I was there, and I didn't realize it either. It's like my Dad used to say, "Dang, Son, It is what it is." Brad and I were going to ride together to Waco, but John rolled into town the night before. He had an appointment scheduled that day and would spend the night and drive to Waco the next morning for the meeting and then drive back through San Antonio on his way home. John called to ask if I was going to the meeting and did I want to ride with him. I told him that Brad and I were riding up together, and he was welcome to ride with us. John sounded mortified that I would suggest that he leave Blackie parked by himself .... uh.... itself. After a short period of him whining and moaning, I agreed to ride with him as long as Brad agreed. I called Brad, and he said he had no real problem with it as long as I promised him no craziness.

Brad had met John a couple of times and had heard all the stories, but he hadn't ever been the victim of one of John's long and loud rants or acting a little strange at times. He is not dangerous; John's just a little quirky. I knew that Brad doesn't do quirky things very well. That's why I was worried.

John picked us up right on time. I herded Brad towards the shotgun position next to John, and I got in the back seat. As it turned out, it appeared I was overreacting a bit because on the drive up, at least, aside from general chit-chat, there wasn't much conversation, probably because it was pretty early since we had to leave around 5:30 in the morning. We made the trip in about two and a half hours and got a big surprise when we turned into the parking lot at the Grand Lodge building and saw it full and guys parked on the surrounding streets. I don't think anyone expected that many Brothers to show up for a special session, but I think it has a lot to do with the enjoyment of getting to see those Brothers that you rarely see except for at Grand Lodge.

It's hard to define exactly, but there is certainly a strong draw for Brothers when they start thinking about going to Grand Lodge. Most everyone managed to get inside the Lodge room before the Grand Master opened, and the business we were there for took a fraction of the time that it took to get all the Brothers registered and into the Lodge room in the first place. As soon as we closed Lodge though, everyone wanted to eat, especially John, and before anyone could make a suggestion, John insisted that we go to Vitec's because, in his opinion, it was the best. Brothers Keith and Burt from our Lodge wanted to go too and were good with wherever we went, and Brad and I had no objections either. So we all piled into our trucks and met at Vitec's BBQ. Without going into a long, drawn-out dissertation on Vitec's virtues, I will simply say that the BBQ there is very, very good. We had all been there before, including John, who everyone in the place seemed to know.

When we walked in the door, Keith and Burt had already finished ordering and were paying for their lunches at the end of the counter. They went to find a table for all of us as we ordered. I was first because I knew that John would not pay for anything, and he did drive all the way. I got a small Gut Buster, a container containing Fritos, cheese, chopped BBQ beef, beans, sausage, pickles, onions, jalapeno peppers, and BBQ sauce. They asked for my name to write on the container and turned to Brad, who ordered next because John was still staring at the overhead menu. Brad got a brisket plate with beans and Coleslaw. While they were handing Brad and I our drink cups, John began to order. I remembered the last time we were here; he got his meal free cause they all knew him. I was hoping that would happen again, but it appeared that was not to be. They didn't seem to know him. It was probably a whole different crew, bummer.

John ordered two large (twice the size of mine) Gut Busters, one with BBQ beef and the other with BBQ pork. The two girls behind the counter were amazed, but he wasn't done yet, sadly for me. He added a BBQ sausage sandwich and a brisket plate. I heard John ask what the side orders were, and the girl said, "beans, Coleslaw, potato salad, and three-cheese macaroni." John nodded and said, "that will do just fine." I almost laughed out loud seeing the blank look on her face, and after a long silence with her and John staring at each other, she said in a small voice, "Which one do you want?" After another pause, John replied with a confused look on his face, "Well Darlin', all of em, of course." It took her a few seconds, but then she got it and got a big smile on her face and asked for his name.

Now, up till now, everything was pretty much OK. I had started moving down the line to pay and pick up our food. Instead of giving his name, I heard John say, "Don't you recognize me?" She looked across at him with a steady gaze, searching his face for something she recognized.

Finally, she smiled, "No." John blinked a couple of times and sounded surprised at her answer, and asked, "Don't you watch Gunsmoke?" Now for all you older Brothers, no explanation is necessary. But for you younger fellers, Gunsmoke was one of the most popular TV Westerns ever made. But noting that the young lady across the counter from us was less than 25 years old, I was pretty sure that not only had she never seen Gunsmoke, she probably never heard of it. I am sure she didn't know that the first episode of Gunsmoke aired in September 1955, and the last was in 1975, probably shortly after her parents were born.

Acting genuinely shocked, John said, "I can't believe that you don't watch Gunsmoke." But, to her credit, trying not to hurt John's feelings, she replied sweetly, "It is just that one that I missed."

"Well, you need to watch it because I am in it," he said. I had stopped moving up the line, waiting to see how far he was going to take this.

"You are?" she asked, with her eyes lighting up with genuine interest.

"Yup," he replied with a big grin. "In the first episode, I was that baby that was crying." I just looked down and shook my head. Surely she was going to call BS on him now. But instead, her smile got bigger as she told him she would call him Mr. Gunsmoke as she wrote it on his container. I looked at him and shook my head again as he followed me down the line with his chest stuck out and a self-satisfied smile on his face.

Out of the corner of my eye, I saw two things: the counter girl telling the other girls behind the counter that John was a celebrity and Brad taking in the whole thing, rolling his eyes at the absurdity of it all. At the cash register, it was more of the same, including me having to pay. Apparently, word travels fast down a serving line because, by the time we got to the register to pay, the words on the gathering group of millennials' lips were "Mr. Gunsmoke." I was already getting tired of that name, but John sure wasn't. I thought that the young lady at the register was exceptionally talented to ring up our order, charge my card, and get my signature on the receipt, all without ever looking at me. *WOW!!* Finally, the "Gunsmoke" show was over, or so I thought.

We made our way back to the table where Keith and Burt were almost finished eating, which was just as well since John needed the extra room for all his food containers. They had observed the drama but couldn't hear what was going on, and after Brad told them what had just happened, Burt just sat there shaking his head while Keith got that mouth open shocked look on his face that anyone who knows him has seen before when he is in total disbelief about what he was hearing. As for me, well, I was used to the weird stuff that happens around John Deacon and was the only one not surprised when seven giggling college girls came over to our table, all wanting an autograph from Mr. Gunsmoke. While we all sat there watching in total disbelief, John graciously signed all the autographs and even posed for a group picture. I guess the most shocking part is that he did all this before he started eating.

Once the groupies were gone, and John did finally start attacking the mountain of grub before him, no sound came from him other than an occasional grunt of pleasure at what he was consuming at the time. We all finished way before John did and took the opportunity of his silence to sincerely and solemnly and with a certain level of sarcasm question his uprightness as a Mason for telling such a tall story to those young girls. John just smiled and winked at us and managed between bites and swallows to pose the question: "How do you fellers know it's not true?"

That shut us up temporarily because I don't think any of us could prove otherwise. I think there was a certain level of jealousy from the other guys (but not me, of course) towards John because he was getting all that positive attention from a host of beautiful young ladies. Finally, John finished, and the show was over except for John, saying goodbye to all his adoring fans. John had to call over his shoulder as we walked out of the door, "Y'all make sure you watch on Tuesday night at 6:30." To which they all chimed in as one...." We will." And so Vitec's was added to the list of eating establishments we could no longer patronize.

I was so glad to get back on the road, and we again rode in silence for the first ten miles or so until I figured I needed to try to extract some Masonic message from John for this month's newsletter. "Hey John," I said from the back seat. "Do you have anything you want to talk about for the newsletter next month?"

There was this long pause like he hadn't heard me, and just as I was going to ask again, John said, "I have this thing that has been on my mind since the Grand Master's conference, and I guess this is as good a time as any to talk about it. As opinionated as most of the Brothers are around the State, you might not want to have this discussion in the newsletter."

"I think Brad and I are pretty free-thinking and open in our views of things," I replied. "So let's give it a try."

"Well, OK then," John began slowly. "I guess it's about time we talked a bit about the Grand Masters recommendation coming up this year."

Uh oh, I thought to myself as I saw Brad shift uncomfortably in the passenger seat. I knew Brad was not on board with that proposal, and I was still on the fence. Maybe this wasn't the right thing for the newsletter after all, but I wanted to hear some discussion about it.

"I don't know how you Brothers feel about this," John continued. "But I have given it a lot of thought while I have been driving by myself around this State. Y'all correct me if I miss something but basically, what I am hearing is that our Grand Master wants to offer a one-time-only opportunity to any Entered Apprentice or Fellow Craft Mason who has gone past the minimum time allowed by law to complete his proficiency in either his first or second degree, to become a Master Mason in one day. Is that the crux of it?"

Out of the corner of my eye, I saw Brad frowning and nodding his head slowly. He wasn't ready to jump into this conversation just yet, but I could tell he was getting close. I jumped in to answer John, "Yes, John, but there are several conditions that apply."

"I realize that, *Brother Chris*," John replied, almost shouting the last two words as a guy in a very tiny car dove in front of us, making John have to brake hard to keep from squashing him. He murmured something under his breath and then took a deep breath and continued, "To start with, any Lodge who has a Brother who meets the qualifications to take advantage of this opportunity can decline to have their Brother EA or FC participate. Secondly, the Brother or Brothers would have to be reinvestigated and found favorable for advancement by their Lodge. If he is found favorable, the Brother would have to pay his degree fee or fees to the Lodge. An EA would see the Fellow Craft degree and the Master's degree exemplified and would be required to learn and demonstrate proficiency in the Masters trial lecture (which to me would test his commitment) and to finish the ALL program within 90 days of his receiving the Masters Degree before becoming a full member."

Brad couldn't hold it any longer and said with as much restraint in his voice that he could muster, "My initial thought is that I am not in favor of this for a couple of reasons I can define and a few more I can't."

"Is part of it about a sense of pride?" John asked, glancing over at Brad. "Knowing every Brother has followed the exact same path as you and that shortcutting the process takes away that pride? Because that's the way, I felt at first. I have said many times in talks to groups of Masons and non-Masons that we all became Masons and took our obligations that same way, and somehow I felt I wouldn't be able to say that anymore."

"Yes, I admit that is part of it,' Brad agreed. "But there is more. I am afraid that it creates two levels of Brothers when we are taught from the beginning that all Masons are on the same level. I am afraid that there will be narrow-minded people who will put Brethren into two categories, those that did and those that didn't. Treat them differently."

Boy, this was shaping up to be a great discussion, and I was not going to interrupt in any way, but just sit in the back and take it all in.

"That's a real good point, my Brother," said John, nodding his head. I thought about that very point for a long, long time. I realize that there are Grand jurisdictions in this country where a man can take all three of his degrees in one day, which is offered regularly. Most don't have to learn any of the esoteric work. Some only have to learn the obligations, but otherwise, they sit and watch the degrees performed in front of them. Being a Texas Mason, that goes against my and our interpretation of what a man must do to become a Mason at heart. But it is not our place or duty to judge other jurisdictions and their laws and regulations. It is always possible that a visiting Brother from another Grand jurisdiction might not have literally traveled the same path as I. It is true that when I meet a visitor, regardless of where or what Grand jurisdiction he is from, I always treat him with the same respect and Brotherly affection as my Brethren.

The truth is that I never pause to consider the possibility that he might have taken a shortcut to becoming a Master Mason, so therefore in the big picture of things, it doesn't matter. What matters is that he is my Brother and is entitled to my trust and respect unless he violates either."

There was total silence inside that truck as we rolled down the highway contemplating John's words. Then, finally, Brad sighed profoundly and, staring straight ahead, said to no one in particular, "Dang it, there is no such thing as an easy decision. Now I just don't know."

"Well, let me throw a little more meat on the fire," John added seriously. I couldn't help wondering why most everything with John had to be about food. God help us if he was hungry again so soon. Thankfully I made it back to reality in time to hear him continue, "I was driving along a long straight stretch of Interstate 20 last week on my way to Amarillo thinking about this whole thing cause I couldn't get it out of my mind. Then out of nowhere, it hit me. It was something that I hadn't even considered. What if the Brother who could have this opportunity to become a Master Mason had not finished his work due to his job changing, a family situation, or maybe a tragedy of some kind? What if that Brother was someone who you knew was a good man and who would benefit from being a Mason and who Masonry would benefit by him being a Mason? What if that Brother was your real Brother, Father, Uncle, or maybe your best friend?"

"You just had to go there, didn't you, John," Brad said with a trace of sarcasm in his voice. You had to state the obvious. But I get the point."

"I'm going to let you in on a Masonic secret, "John said so quietly that I had to lean forward to hear. "It's something you both already know. Several Brethren within our Fraternity never were, aren't now, and never will be true and upright Brothers. At the same time, many men have taken the first and some the first and second degrees in Masonry who have the purity of heart and uprightness of conduct that would make them great Masons. Why should they not have an opportunity to become a Master Mason to learn from Masons, Freemasonry, and live Masonic life?

Now, no matter what is said, there will be Brothers out there who will never hope to give anyone a chance to become a Master Mason in this Grand jurisdiction without fulfilling every requirement that he had to do. I only wish there are more out there who are open-minded enough to see this for what it is. I don't think this is intended as an easy way out for these Brothers because there are pretty strict guidelines to qualify for this opportunity. There are also consequences for failure to follow the guidelines. You know the guidelines, don't you?"

Brad looked over at John and said, "It's pretty simple, really. If, after a Brother looking to take advantage of this program pays his money and shows up to the Degrees and fulfills all of what is required of him, but fails to learn and be examined as to his proficiency in the Masters work, and or he fails to complete the ALL program within ninety days he is automatically suspended. Is that pretty much it?"

"Yup," said John, nodding his ascent. "That is it as I understand it. But there is more to consider, especially for those Brothers who still have trouble accepting it. Suppose a Brother fulfills all the requirements of this one-time program and becomes nothing more than a card-carrying Mason. A Mason in name only he will be no worse or better than 50% of the members in the Fraternity now. However, if he should become an active Brother, he will surely become a part of working in the degrees and will also at some point want to teach and pass along our lessons to new Brothers. To do this, he will have to learn all the work of all the other degrees that he didn't when he was made a Master Mason. Knowing what I know about the beauty of our degrees, there will come a time when most, if not all, of these new Brothers will wish they had received their Masters degree the way the rest of us did."

"But John," interjected Brad, who for some strange reason didn't have to endure the John Deacon glare for interrupting. "Don't you think this is all about membership numbers and money?"

"Many will say exactly that," chuckled John, shaking his head. No one should be so naïve as to think that money and membership aren't a big part of it. Heck, we spent the last aren't years at least with (as my Dad used to say) our heads where the sun doesn't shine and have allowed what is arguably one of the most historically significant buildings built in the last century in Texas to begin to crumble around us without realizing what was happening to us and our Fraternity. Here we are, many days late and three million dollars short, trying to find a way to fix it because we have no choice. If I have to explain to you, Brothers, why we have no choice, I will let both of you out on the side of the road right now. But I believe it also has a lot to do with allowing Brothers to fulfill their Masonic dream. For some, it is the only way it can ever happen. I hear that Oklahoma did this one year and got not only a few hundred new Master Masons, but years later, one who took advantage of the program became their Grand Master. I genuinely believe that the good things that will come out of this far outweigh any negatives there might be."

Just then, we pulled into the parking lot where we left our trucks, and as I sat there in the back seat, I saw Brad smile and his hand reach across to shake John's, and yes, it was a grip that held much significance for all of us.

No more words were spoken as we silently communicated our goodbyes. There was no reason for words. Everything had been said. As I pointed my truck towards home, the thought came to me that the article's name is the *Profound Pontifications,* and there indeed were plenty of profundities emanating from the big guy today. I sure hoped that when I wrote it down, I could communicate it with the same passion as John did, and I hope it stirs some thought within each of you.

Val, The Ring and the Fork

We just finished a fabulous meal, and I was hoping John was ready to talk. So far, nothing crazy has happened, and with a bit of luck, we might get out of here without anything weird catching up to us. I brought John back to Maggiano's. Thankfully this time, we weren't crashing a wedding. Nope, I brought him to meet Val.

Now who, you ask, is Val? Pam and I come here at least once a week, and we always sit in the bar area and only where Val will be our server. We have been coming to Maggiano's for several years, and for us, it is what it is because of Val. Val is, of course, short for Valerie, and although the food is fabulous, if it were not the best, we would still come because of her. Yes, this is our place, and she, along with Will, Becky, Cynthia, and all the others, makes the experience the best it can be.

John had, as usual, ordered almost everything on the menu: Lasagna, fried zucchini, cheese ravioli, Chicken Alfredo, and Chicken Piccata. All with generous amounts of warm bread and Caesar salad. I ordered Lasagna and a salad. It was all I could eat. So there we were, just basking in the warmth and fuzzy that comes with a full stomach.

"Brother Chris," John asked slowly. "Have you ever had something happen to you that you couldn't explain? Something so profound that it changed forever the way you thought about things? Maybe something that just had to be the work of the Great Architect of the Universe?"

"Actually, I ha..." I tried to respond as John cut me off. Obviously, he did not expect nor want an answer.

"This is one of my favorite stories, and I don't tell it often, but sometimes it is just the right time," John said, pulling several folded pages out of his shirt pocket and beginning to read. "This story begins with a Brother Mason who was on his deathbed; he knew his earthly life was about over. His family gathered around his bed, wanting to be with him until the end. The Brother asked for one of his daughters, and when she bent close, he whispered to her a dying man's request that she make sure that her son, his Grandson, would someday become a Freemason. She readily made the promise to him as any good daughter would, he smiled, and then he was gone.

The next day a six-year-old boy was presented with a cardboard box by his mother. The box contained several books with some unusual markings and pictures, a Bible, a funny cocked hat, and a sword with some of the same markings. He was as aware as a six-year-old boy can be that his Grandfather had gone to be with the angels, and he would never see him again.

Standing there, a little bewildered, his mother told him that the box was from his Grandfather and that he had wanted his Grandson to be a Freemason someday. The boy nodded without understanding why and took the box to his room, where it stayed for the next 16 years. During those years as he was growing up, the boy often saw the box packed away in the back of his closet. He didn't think too much about it or the promise his mother had made to his Grandfather.

Eventually, he moved out of the house, and along with all of his belongings, the box went with him. It wasn't long before he was married, and at one point, his wife had seen and asked about the old, now tattered box. The young man mumbled something about his Grandfather had given it to him. He did not explain that the box with its contents and the promise went unfulfilled for many years until one day the Grandson met a man who was a salesman. The salesman was calling on the business where the Grandson worked. As the salesman spoke, the Grandson noticed an unusual symbol on the ring that the salesman was wearing, and he realized that it was one of the same symbols he had seen on the books in the box his Grandfather had given him all those years ago. The Grandson inquired about it and found out that the man was a member of a fraternity called the Freemasons. He asked the man to tell him about the mysterious organization. As the man talked, the Grandson began, for the first time, to gain a glimmer of understanding of what his Grandfather had been a part of so many years ago. More importantly, he began to understand why. That conversation led to more discussions which led to a friendship. That friendship led the Grandson to at last fulfill his Grandfather's dying wish and become a Freemason.

Over the next 15 years, he grew as a man and a Mason and eventually became Worshipful Master of his Lodge. Upon completing his year in the East, he became interested in his Grandfather's Masonic career, searching to find his Lodge and information about him Masonically. He knew that he was a good man from his mother and the rest of the family, but he wanted to connect with him, to get to know him, Brother to Brother, as only a shared Masonic experience can do.

That search turned up much information, including the fact that the Grandfather had been Master of his Lodge. He had also served as The Secretary for many years. This information was provided by the Secretary of his Grandfather's Lodge, who was happy to chart the Grandfather's Masonic journey.

The Secretary invited the Grandson to visit the Lodge where his Grandfather's picture was hanging proudly on the wall of the Lodge room with the other Past Masters. The visit was an emotional one for the Grandson. He saw the picture hanging in the North part of the Lodge room and had the opportunity to view the minutes of meetings of the Lodge, which bore the signature of his Grandfather as Worshipful Master that was over 75 years old. From that moment on, the association with the Secretary became a close Masonic friendship, and they continued to stay in touch.

It was just about a year later when the Grandson opened an email from the Secretary asking him, "what would you say if I told you that I know where your Grandfather's Masonic ring is?"

Since being made a Mason, and knowing that almost every Mason wore a Masonic ring, the Grandson had often wondered what happened to his Grandfather's ring after his death. It was not in the tattered cardboard box he had finally gone through and lovingly touched and carefully placed each item in its special place in his office. Instead, he had all but forgotten about it long ago, surmising that it had been left on the finger it had occupied for 25 years before laying down the working tools of life.

The emotions stirred by the Secretary's revelation were hard to suppress, and it took several minutes to respond. When he did, it was that "he had no words to express the emotion he felt at this news."

The quick reply by the Secretary, "My Brother, if you have ever wondered if the Great Architect was truly guiding our way through this middle chamber of life, then you had better call me because I am about to dispel any doubts."

The Grandson dialed the familiar number with a shaky hand, and the call was answered before the first ring was finished. Barely able to control his excitement, the Secretary said that he had an amazing story to tell him. He said that two days before, the Lodge had held a BBQ fundraiser on a Saturday, and it had just ended for the day. The Brothers of the Lodge and the Eastern Star were cleaning up after the event.

While sitting at his Secretary's desk in the Lodge, the only other people in the Lodge were the Worshipful Master and his wife. The two talked to each other, standing next to the Junior Warden's station in the South directly opposite where the Grandfather's picture hung in the North. As he was working on Lodge paperwork, he said that he heard the wife ask her husband the WM, "Did you ever know Blaine Price?" The Secretary, realizing that she had just used the name of the Grandfather he had researched for the Grandson and that the question seemingly came out of nowhere, forced him to look up quickly, just in time to see the completely confused look on the Worshipful Master's face. He had no clue who she was talking about nor where the question came from.

The Worshipful Master shook his head and told her that he had never met him. She then told her husband that her father had been Brother Price's mentor in Masonry and that they had worked together at the Fire Dept. She said that after Brother Price's death, his widow had given his Masonic ring to her father, who had bequeathed it to her, and that after all those years, she still had it. She said that she remembered Brother Price and the times he would come to her house to talk to her father and the strong bond they seemed to have.

The Secretary told the Grandson that he sprang out of his chair and covered the few feet between his desk and the South station at almost a run upon hearing this. He confronted the surprised woman and asked her what had made her ask that question about Brother Price? She thought for a second or two and replied that she didn't know that it had just popped into her mind right at that moment.

The Secretary then proceeded to tell her the story of the Grandson who had contacted him and of his visit to the Lodge. He said at that moment she got a funny look on her face and turned to look at the North wall and that he and the WM, having the same thought, looked around to where the picture was hanging in the North half expecting to see Brother Price standing there.

The Secretary said that he was, at that moment, as the hair on the back of his neck was standing up, convinced that this long-departed Brother had somehow picked the right time, with the right people, in the right place, to make sure that his most treasured Masonic possession, his Masonic ring, could find its way to the person he wanted to have it. The wife immediately said that she wanted to give it to the Grandson with tears in her eyes.

The Grandson, hearing all of this, had tears streaming down his cheeks. He was completely convinced that his Grandfather working through the guiding influence of the Great Architect of the Universe, had found a way to connect with him through the shared love and understanding of the true meaning of our Masonic Fraternity and our Brotherly love and affection of one another. He realized that the connection with his Grandfather that he had been seeking had just happened, and he would be forever changed by it."

I noticed as John read, his voice got softer and softer, and by the end, it was almost hoarse. John got quiet, and I instinctively knew that I needed to wait quietly. After a couple of minutes, he continued, "Brother Chris, there is no doubt in my mind that what happened here was meant to happen, that it was probably written a long time ago. It may be part of a larger plan, a plan that has yet to reveal itself."

Then John stopped and I, exposing myself to John Deacon's scorn for interrupting, said in a whisper, (why was I whispering, I have no clue) "John, that was an amazing story. Where did you get that?"

He looked up, and as we locked eyes, I could tell his eyes were wet. As he wiped away a tear with the back of his hand, he pulled something off the little finger of his left hand and reached across the table, and handed it to me. As I stared at it with my mouth hanging open, I asked with a barely audible voice, "Is this it, John. Is this your Grandfather's ring?" I looked up as he wiped away another tear and nodded slowly.

"Wow, John," I exclaimed! "I had no idea as you read that. What a beautiful story. It is beautifully written too. Did you write it? I have no words except wow!"

"Heck, yes, I wrote it," he said stiffly. "You think you are the only one who can write stuff down? Actually, I tried to write it the way you would."

"Well, it was great!"

John smiled and said softly, "After this, I do not believe in luck or coincidence anymore. I now know that wherever I am, is where I am supposed to be. Whatever happens, is what is supposed to happen. When I stopped looking at what was right in front of me and instead stepped back and broadened my view, I can now see beyond what is readily apparent. I can see much more than I did before and understand much more than I did before. The Great Architect is always guiding us. The choice we all have is to fight his guidance or relax and go with him. It does not mean that we should sit back and wait for Him to show us what to do. We alone are responsible for our lives and how we live them. He leads us to a fork in the road every day and sometimes several times a day where we have to decide right or wrong. We know the right decision almost every time, yet we still make the wrong one many times, but He never gives up on us. He always has confidence in us, and He leads us back to that fork and gives us another chance."

John smiled and slid out of the booth. He stuck out his massive hand, and I gripped it. Yes, with the firm grip of a Master Mason. He said, "Brother Chris, my Grandfather found me, and he gave me his ring. Nothing could be more Masonically special than that. I will never be the same."

As he turned and walked out the door, I couldn't help but wipe away a tear as I whispered, "I love you, my Brother John. God bless you, my friend."

Allen's, Sweetwater and A Mystical Perception

It was a Friday a few weeks ago. I was on my way to Lubbock, Texas, to a weekend training conference with some other Education and Service Committee members. Larry, our Chairman, was heading the same way, just from a different direction. He was bringing two other committee members, Richard and Lane. Realizing that our routes were going to join in a little town called Sweetwater, and pretty close to lunch time, we decided to meet there and have some lunch. There we could do a little planning for the weekend ahead before driving the last leg into Lubbock. We had sought that learned sage Uncle Google's advice and found out that the best place to eat in the area was Allen's Home Style restaurant located just east of beautiful downtown Sweetwater, Texas. So that seeming like our best option, we decided to meet there around noon.

I got there about 45 minutes before they did, and since I was unfamiliar with the town, I figured I would locate this Allen's Home Style restaurant and make it easier for them to find when they got in. So I entered the address into my GPS and proceeded to the highlighted route where the guidance system took over; sounds familiar, huh? As it turned out, I didn't need the navigation system because it looked like every vehicle in Sweetwater was parked at Allen's. I thought, *wow, it looks like we picked the right place for sure.*

I called Larry and told him how to get to the restaurant and told him I would see if I could find an antique shop to look through while I waited. He threatened me about buying "all the good stuff," he was still hurling threats as I hung up on him. Larry and I are on the same page when it comes to old Masonic stuff.

I conversed briefly with my favorite Uncle Google again to ascertain the whereabouts of any antique shops in Sweetwater and got four possibilities. I have been fortunate in the past to find some old and rare Masonic jewelry as well as some old books. All of the shops happened to be located on the same street, and all were closed except one. I parked and walked in. I was greeted by the owner and his wife, who told me to take my time and look around. I said that I didn't have a lot of time, but I was looking to see if they had anything Masonic in the store. Immediately I got the feeling that I had said something wrong. He and his wife looked at each other and then everywhere but at me. It was like I was a DEA agent, and they were drug kingpins. They seemed as guilty (about something) as I've ever seen anyone. I was baffled and asked, "What's wrong?" Looking from side to side like he didn't want anyone to hear (there was no one else in the store), he leaned across the counter towards me and said in a low voice, "I do have a few things, but I can't let anyone see them until the Mayor sees them first."

I didn't know how to respond to that. I just stood there with my mouth hanging open, trying to figure out what I had missed. A lot of things flashed by in my mind did this town have a problem with Freemasons? Was I in some kind of danger? The hair stood up on the back of my neck as I watched his hands to see if he pressed a hidden button under the counter. Or did they have something really valuable and special? Or maybe, Brad is right when he says I am such a drama queen. Well, that may be, but this was still a little weird.

There we were staring at each other across the counter when the voice broke the silence of reason, aka his wife saying, "Yes, the Mayor is the Master of the local Masonic Lodge, and he has first dibs on all Mason stuff." "Ahhhh!" I said, the light finally shining in. "I totally understand now. He is not only a good man but a smart man as well." As they nodded in agreement, I thanked them and took my leave from the little antique shop on the corner of Main Street.

I decided to go back to Allen's and wait for the guys to show up. It was close to one o'clock when I got there, and most of the cars had cleared out, so I took a spot in the front row. I wasn't sitting there for more than five minutes when Larry's Tahoe pulled in and parked next to me. We all piled out of our trucks and threw the usual pleasantries and insults at each other, and headed for the front door of Allen's.

The minute we walked in the door, we were confronted, and I do not mean greeted; I do mean confronted by a woman who demanded to know how many were in my party. Startled, I quickly said four, and she pointed to a table for ten that had three guys already sitting at it and said, "Sit there." Not even looking at who we were going to be sitting with, I glanced around at the room and saw that there were seven other tables, all of which were empty. I was confused, and by the look on Larry's and the other guys' faces, they were too, but before I could ask why, the woman ordered us again to sit.

Now, I don't know about you, dear Reader, but I am married and have been for 41 years, and unless my life is in jeopardy when a woman says sit, I usually sit and ask questions later.

Apparently, Larry, Richard, and Lane had been trained in the same tradition. As we sat, she asked what we wanted to drink, suggesting iced tea, and by the time our rear ends hit the chair, there were drinks already in front of us. If everything hadn't gone fast enough already, it got even faster as several women started placing platters and bowls of food on the table in front of us. We were still in stunned mode and watched as each bowl and platter was picked up as soon as it hit the table by the guys across from us, and after shoveling some onto their plates, they passed them down. Eventually, each platter and bowl made its way around the table to us, where we likewise took some for ourselves. There was a platter piled high with fresh hot fried chicken (the best I have ever had) and another with half-inch slabs of roast beef. There were bowls with what looked like every kind of vegetable known to man. As they passed into and out of my hands, I saw mashed potatoes, potato salad, green beans, collard greens, red beans, cabbage, freshly boiled okra, creamed corn, mac and cheese, carrots, squash and gravy, and fresh rolls. There were a couple of things I could not identify but tasted good. At that point, there was nothing left to do but dig in and eat, and we did.

I had totally forgotten that we were sitting across from three other guys, and when I heard his voice, I froze for a split second before looking up. When I did, I was staring into the big blue eyes of THE Big John Deacon. I just smiled and stood up, as did he, and met him at the head of the table. Our right hands clasped in that familiar grip embracing each other with the other. It had been more than a year since I had seen him, and other than looking like he had gained a few pounds, he looked the same. Realizing, I suppose, that food was on the table and getting cold, he broke away abruptly and went back to his seat.

As I sat down, he reached across the table, greeted Larry, Richard, and Lane, and introduced his two friends who were not members of the Fraternity. "I thought you were retired," I said to him as he filled his mouth with a sizable fork full of food. John tried to answer but was waived off by everyone at the table at the sight of him trying to talk with a full mouth.

One of his companions, Mark, replied that "He was, but they brought him out of retirement so he could show Bill and me the territory."

Then John, making a big deal out of swallowing, added, "Naaah, I am just showing these fellers all the best places to eat." Now, that is something I could believe for sure.

"And I'll bet you are sticking your two buddies with your lunch bill like you used to with me," I shot at him. As I said that, I could see the two heads on either side of him nodding in agreement. "He used to justify sticking me with buying his lunch," I continued looking at Mark, "by telling me that the wisdom he was giving me was worth every penny." As I said that, the two turned to stare at John, who flushed slightly but kept on eating.

Finally, we all settled into just enjoying the meal. There wasn't much conversation except for requests for more of this or that every time a bowl or platter got emptied. I watched, amazed at the mountain of chicken bones on the plate next to John. Every time a bowl or platter was emptied, it was replaced immediately with another full one, and usually, it didn't have time to touch the table before John grabbed it and forked, scooped, or poured the majority of its contents on his plate. Wow, some things never change. As I sat there watching John, I realized with satisfaction how un-stressful this meal was, since I didn't have to pay for John's lunch and I wasn't trying to meet a deadline on writing his words of wisdom in time to get it in a newsletter. So unless he were feeling particularly talkative, there would be no profound pontifications today… and that was ok with me.

Larry, seeing how much food was being consumed and the unique situation we were in and John sitting right across the table from us, elbowed me and whispered, "Wow, this would make a heck of a John Deacon article." He was right, but the key was and has always been whether and what he has to say. Sometimes what he says is unprintable, and sometimes it is un-understandable, and then other times, it is just a lot of whining and moaning. The truth was that right now; I was hoping he didn't have anything to say. But time would tell as it looked like he was starting to get full. I know I felt like I was about to pop, so I pushed my plate away and leaned back, and took a deep breath.

John saw my discomfort and grinned, "You think you are done eating, Brother Chris?"

"No," I answered, not even attempting to hide my pain. "I don't just think I am done; I know I am done."

John, still grinning, said, "Just wait." As he said those words, the smell of something familiar floated across the table, something I really liked. Before I could say it out loud, four bowls of warm fresh homemade peach cobbler were laid on the table.

The first two bowls were empty before they left John's hands, and the next two were empty before they got to me. Then came two more and the third two bowls. I grabbed one, and Lane grabbed the other, and between the two of us, Larry and Richard finally got some cobbler too. Then once again, silence descended, and before it was over, there were four more bowls of cobbler delivered to our table. I had two helpings, and I was sure I was going to be sick from overeating, but all John could say was, "Told you so." But it was some of the best peach cobbler I have ever had.

I had eaten so much I thought I might lose consciousness. I couldn't remember ever feeling as miserable as I did and at the same time satisfied by the incredible food, and when I glanced around, it looked like everyone at the table was in the same shape I was. I remember my grandfather used to lean back in his chair after a big meal and say to no one in particular, "I think I feel a nap coming on." I used to laugh at him when he would say that, but now I know that he was a very wise man. However, a nap was not in my immediate future.

All of a sudden, John's voice broke the silence. He suddenly felt it necessary to expound to all of us his view of life and the world about us. He announced to everyone within hearing that he was in the process of expanding his mind. Before I could stop it from coming out of my mouth, I mumbled something about, "that's not the only thing that is expanding." We all had to endure a ten-second John Deacon glare while choking on our laughter before he went on. He said that many things are happening around us that we do not realize or even think about. He said that we need to make our view wider and not just see what is in front of us. He said that he had been reading a lot about Brother Manly P. Hall and that Brother Hall had stated that "It is said that wisdom lies not in seeing things, but in seeing *through* things.

"Daaaang Brother John," I said approvingly. "You sound like you have turned into some kind of Mystic or something."

"Brother Chris," he replied, looking a little puzzled. "I don't really know what a Miss Stick or even a Mr. Stick or any other kind of stick or whatever the heck you are trying to say is… all I really know is that I am looking at things a little bit different lately. It's like things are sending me out a lot bigger messages than they ever have before."

Everyone was chuckling at his "Miss Stick/Mr. Stick" reference, and the guy sitting on his left decided to take it a step further and said to John, "Do you have to wear your little tin foil cap to tune in to all those messages?" Then he threw back his head and laughed out loud. However, when he opened his eyes, four Brother Masons were not laughing, staring daggers at him. With a look of confusion and fear on his face, the laughter abruptly stopped.

John looked directly at the three of us and said in a serious voice, "I want to tell you what happened last week in Lodge. We were about halfway through our Stated Meeting when the Worshipful Master stood up and said he needed to make an announcement. He said that the week before, one of the Lodge Brothers had given him a gift. Well, right there, I started to think that the middle of a stated Meeting might not be the best place to talk about something personal that happened between the Worshipful Master and another Brother. But it turned out that he had a good reason for sharing it with all of us.

He said that the gift was something of considerable value and that he was very touched by the Brother's desire to present it to him. He said that the gift had a note accompanying it, and the message said thanks for being a friend and mentor to Brother's many years and for all the things he had taught him. As he told us this, the Worshipful Master got a little emotional and had to clear his throat a couple of times. It was then that he commenced making his point.

He said that it had never dawned on him that he was doing the things that the Brother was thanking him for and that it had made him realize that as Masons, "we don't sometimes realize what we do for others." The Lodge got real quiet as all the Brothers there contemplated that statement," ....and

John grinned as he glanced at the three of us, "just like all of you are doing right now."

"Now there was a time," John continued, "when I would just take that statement as face value and not give it much thought, but this is the new and improved John." We all snorted and shook our heads and quickly agreed that we saw nothing new or improved across the table from us, and we told him so.

John glared and ignored us and went on with his story. "On the way home that night, I couldn't stop thinking about what the Worshipful Master had said. I started thinking about how important it is that we as Masons commit ourselves to being good men and doing the right thing, and without realizing it, our conduct probably does affect those around us. Heck, if you belong to an organization that says to everyone that we take good men and make them better, people will probably be eyeballing us to see if we are who we say we are.

As I was driving down that road, I recollected a time I read a paper where it pretty much proved that this great Country was created based upon the principles and teachings of this Fraternity. Yet there was no mention anywhere of our Fraternity as having anything to do with this Country's founding. History also fails to mention that almost all the major newspapers in the colonies at the time were owned and operated by Masons. Nor is it written in any historical account of the founding of our Country that a large percentage of the men who signed the Declaration of Independence, those who wrote the Constitution, as well as those who were the leaders of our Federal government were our Brother Freemasons."

"I think that most of us at this table would agree with that, John," I interrupted, having forgotten the perils of doing so. "But how does that have anything to do with your story about your Worshipful Master?"

There was a silence...a too long silence...an uncomfortable silence accompanied by John's death stare. I had forgotten how bad John hated to be interrupted, and I have found that the best thing to do is be silent till he gets his thoughts back together because that usually takes a little while.

Finally, he got it together and continued as if he had never stopped, "The point is my pain in the rear Brother Chris, that since there was no evidence anywhere that our Masonic Fraternity organized or led the revolution and yet the facts are there that our Country was in fact founded on Masonic principles, then it follows that the Masons of the thirteen colonies, and there were very few of them, by communicating and living those principles and tenets, influenced not only the revolution but also the writing of our Constitution and the formation of the government. Therein lies my point, and it is in the words that the Worshipful Master spoke. '*We really don't realize what we do for others*' or how much living our lives as true Masons influences those around us. And that is something we need to think about every day."

John stopped talking and let us contemplate in silence what he had just said. Naaaah, that's not true. Actually, he noticed a tiny bit of peach cobbler left in the bottom of one of the bowls and proceeded to scrape a couple of layers of paint off the bowl, trying to get that last molecule out of it. But it did silence us and made us think. Even the two non- Masons at the table were left speechless.

As I sat there allowing the warm feeling of his words wash over us, it occurred to me that any good things that we do or any good things that others see in us that would influence them to emulate us, has to come as a result of not just being a member of this Fraternity, but by BEING a Mason and also understanding what a Mason really is and what Masonry is really about. Only then can Masons and Masonry have a natural effect on people and society.

The name *Freemason* is not enough. There are way too many named (and many come to mind as I sat there) organizations and groups whose actions are contrary to what their name or stated purpose implies. The name means nothing unless the actions meet or exceed it. The majority of things that we do, we do without thinking about them and as such are the products of the good men that we are, but those times that we come to that fork in the road where we are challenged to do something different. React differently from most people would; those are the times that show the world the true meaning of being a Freemason. John's Worshipful Master obviously had been a great example of Masonry to his Brother, and I expect that he was the same everywhere.

I snapped back into the present at the sound of dishes clattering, and not surprisingly, John was busy making sure there was nothing left in any. Finally, Larry announced that we needed to get back on the road on my left, and he was right. We had taken a lot longer than we planned for lunch. I asked for the bill, but the lady clearing off the table informed us that there was none and to go to the register.

I do not know how I managed to pull myself to my feet, it sure wasn't easy, but it was gratifying to see that I wasn't the only one with that problem. I was the first to stagger to the cashier, and I started to tell her what I had eaten, and she ignored me and simply said, "Ten dollars" I couldn't believe what I was hearing. I had my wallet in my hands, and as I opened it, I asked, "Ten Dollars?" Obviously, she didn't have the time or patience to explain it to me as she reached into my opened wallet and deftly extracted a ten-dollar bill, slid it into the register, and thanked me all in the same motion. All the guys were in line behind me, and it was apparent that everyone thought I was shocked by how inexpensive the meal was; however, the truth was that I was angry.

How could you be angry, you say? I was mad for several reasons. First, I was mad because of all the lunches I had endured with John that he had eaten enough food for four grown men and stuck me with the check. Second, I was angry that here I was at the same lunch with John Deacon, and all he had eaten was only going to cost his two groupies ten lousy dollars. Wow, I needed to get on the road and cool off. I got out to my truck, and before I could open the door, I was stopped in my tracks by the booming voice of John as he ran across the parking lot to my truck. He was pretty winded, having run about 30 feet, and I thought he might have a heart attack as he reached out and grabbed me in one of those smothering John Deacon bear hugs.

"I haven't seen you for over a year, my Brother pardner. Let's not make it so long next time."

Well, I forgot about being angry and said, "I agree, John" and hugged him back even though I couldn't come close to getting my arms around what can only be described as his equator. I am sure some people were scandalized watching two grown men hug, but there is much meaning in a Masonic embrace. That is all I am going to say about that...

Sitting in my truck waiting for Larry to go in front of me, I watched John haul his humongous -ness into the driver's seat of Ol Blackie, and I smiled at his name for that big black truck.

As he roared off down the road, I was angry again about that dang ten dollars. I hope I can get over that before I see him again.

THE PROFUNDITIES END

After nine years and over 90 articles, my Brother John Deacon is retiring. And since he won't be traveling around the great State of Texas selling those *Working Tools* as he calls them, I won't be seeing him regularly, if at all. That is not to say that our paths won't cross at a Masonic function somewhere, sometime in this Grand Jurisdiction. If he shares some profundity worthy of repeating and he doesn't embarrass me too much, I might be inclined to share it with everyone.

Big John is not dead......just taking a much-needed rest. I am sure he has plenty more to say. As much of a pain in the rear as he has been to me, I love him dearly and will forever appreciate his words of education, wisdom, and inspiration. Writing his words has been both enlightening and therapeutic. I will miss it greatly.

On the other hand, not having to endure paying the bill for our monthly lunches will save me a lot of money. Pam still thinks I buy lunch for five guys instead of one every month. When I started writing these monthly articles nine years ago, I never expected to be doing it for more than one or two years, much less nine. I never expected these stories meant for my Brothers at Davy Crockett Lodge to be published in a four-book series. It was, every minute, truly a labor of love, and although a heck of a lot of work, I have enjoyed every minute of the time creating them.

I want to thank the many contributors of information over the years. I also want to thank all of my Brothers, friends, and family who have been steady and loyal readers of *The Profound Pontifications of Brother John Deacon* since the beginning. Without you and your constant words of encouragement and support, I could not have kept this going for all these years. I hope that something John said spoke to you personally and may have caused you to give the topic or idea some serious thought. Thank you all again for reading our words—Adios for now from John and me.

The End…

A Note to the Reader

Thank you for purchasing and reading my book! I hope that this book has inspired you and has become a valuable addition to your Masonic library. If you have enjoyed this book, please consider leaving an honest review on your favorite online bookstore website.

As a special thank you for reading this book, please head to www.perfectashlarpublishing.com to access free content and to stay up-to-date with our latest news.

Don't forget to pick up each copy of the John Deacon series:

The Profound Philosophical Pontifications of Big John Deacon, Freemason Extraordinaire

Volume I: March 2021

Volume II: April 2021

Volume III: June 2021

Volume IV: September 2021

ABOUT THE AUTHOR

Brother James Christie (Chris) Williams IV was born in Mesa, Arizona, on a working cow ranch. During his younger years, he and his family moved to Texas, back to Arizona, and then finally back to San Antonio, Texas, where he resides with his wife of 45 years. He is very devoted to his daughter, son, and grandchildren and loves spending time with them and his several nieces.

Brother Chris loves Freemasonry and is very devoted to the Craft. He is Past Master of Davy Crockett Lodge No. 1225 in San Antonio and a member of several other Lodges. He holds membership in the Scottish Rite Valley of San Antonio, the York Rite, and the Shrine.

As a member of the Grand Lodge of Texas Masonic Education and Service Committee, Brother Chris has, for the last ten years, assisted in the instruction of prospective officers in revitalizing, administering, and managing their Lodges. He has spoken at Lodges and Masonic gatherings all over Texas on various topics from History to Grand Lodge Law to our Degrees' philosophy and symbolism and much more. He has an enduring love of Masonic Education and is committed to spreading Masonic light whenever and wherever possible.

A NOTE TO THE READER

Thank you for purchasing and reading my book! I hope that this book has inspired you and has become a valuable addition to your Masonic library. If you have enjoyed this book, please consider leaving an honest review on your favorite online bookstore website.

As a special thank you for reading this book, please head to www.perfectashlarpublishing.com to access free content and to stay up to date with our latest news.

Check out these Masonic books from Perfect Ashlar Publishing

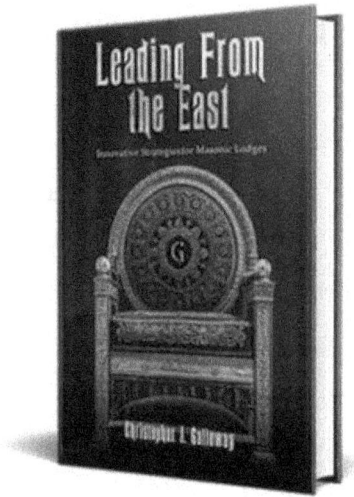

Leading from the East: Innovative Strategies for Masonic Lodges

By Christophor J. Galloway, PM

For over 200 years, Masonic scholars have written about the need for innovation in Freemasonry to "save our fraternity." Within the pages of Leading From the East, resources and strategies will help Blue Lodge leaders identify their vision, attract new members from several different generations, and engage the new members who join. Additionally, the very same strategies will bring back those Brothers who have disengaged from our Craft. A Worshipful Master implemented the strategies presented in this book at a Blue Lodge that was in jeopardy of closing its doors forever and now that same lodge has a bright future. Finally, this book is also a call to action that Masonic leaders must take a new approach to keep Freemasonry around for another 300 years.

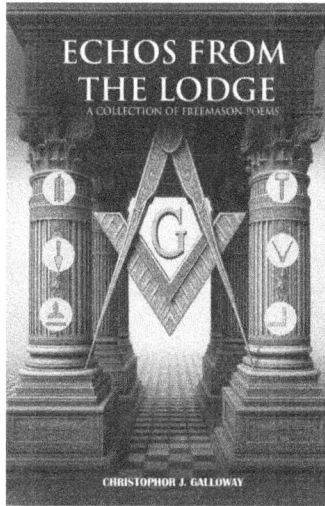

Echos From the Lodge

A Collection of Freemason Poems

By Christophor J. Galloway, PM

Journey into the world of Freemasonry through the poetic artistry of Christophor J. Galloway, Past Master. "Echos from the Lodge" unveils the profound wisdom, rich traditions, and timeless values of the Masonic Brotherhood. In this evocative collection, each poem captures the essence of Masonic life, from the solemn rites and symbols to the bonds of brotherhood that unite Masons across generations. With themes of charity, truth, and the pursuit of knowledge, Galloway's verses resonate with the echos of ancient lodges and the whispered secrets of the Craft.

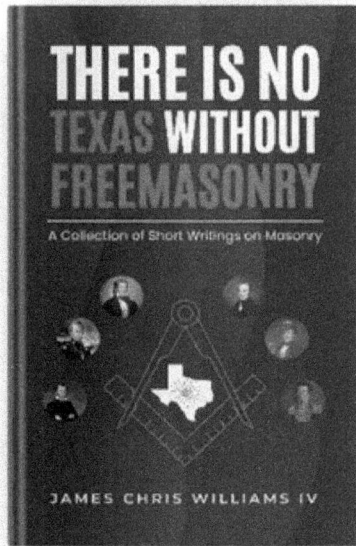

There is No Texas Without Freemasonry: A Collection of Short Writings on Masonry

By James "Chris" Williams IV, PM

Within the covers of this book is a collection of Masonic papers written over the last twenty-five years by Brother Williams. Most of them have been presented at various Masonic and non- Masonic gatherings. There is No Texas Without Freemasonry is the first and most famous paper presented to date by Brother Williams. This book is an excellent addition to any Masonic library. Each chapter is short enough to be read as an education piece in the Lodge or as the focus of family education night. Enjoy each page as you laugh, cry, and, more importantly, reflect on Freemasonry.

Light Reflections: Philosophical Thoughts and Observations of a Texas Freemason

By Bradley E. Kohanke, PM

Freemasonry in the United States was arguably at its peak during the decade following the first World War. The Masonic writings of the day were eloquent, easy to read, concise, and filled with thought-provoking opinions and observations. This was the model after which Bradley E. Kohanke patterned his writings. For nearly 10 years, Brother Kohanke, a Past Master, former District Deputy Grand Master, and former Grand Orator for the Grand Lodge of Texas wrote a monthly article for his Lodge's newsletter.

Also included are his Orations from the Texas Grand Lodge Historical Observances in 2019 and his Grand Oration from the Grand Annual Communication in January of 2020. As Brother Kohanke puts it:

Masonry holds no secrets or sacred knowledge that are suddenly revealed to the initiate. Rather, it provides a framework on which to build…a guide for living. It offers a way to attain that knowledge over time through learning, patience, and truth. And it does so without harming others in their search. This practice of perfecting one's self is ancient beyond record and is the true measure of success. The attainment of balance in one's life…achieving happiness with yourself, without interfering with the happiness of others, and proactively helping others in their search for balance in their lives…that is success.

It is a noble quest, the objective of which can only truly be obtained by those who are worthy and true…to themselves and each other. Good luck on your quest, and enjoy it.

"Masonic duty is to learn and to teach others."

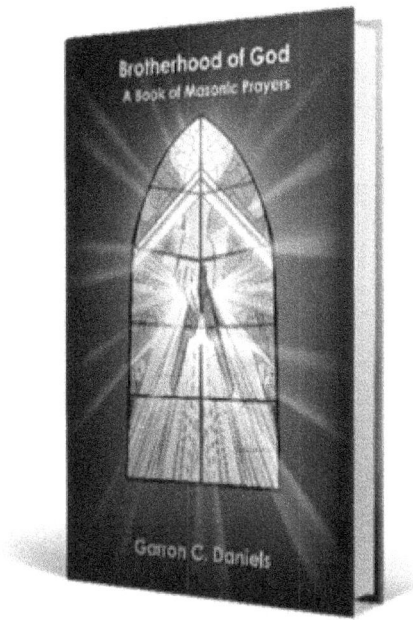

Brotherhood of God:

A Book of Masonic Prayers

By Garron C. Daniels

Brotherhood of God is a collection of prayers to be used by Freemasons, used both within the Lodge and in daily life. It is an aid for the spiritual needs of the Fraternity to remind all of the importance of God in all that we do.

Garron C. Daniels is a Freemason from the State of Missouri. He's a member of Brotherhood Lodge #269 in St Joseph, Mo, a member of the Scottish Rite and York Rite, and several other fundraising bodies of Freemasonry.

He gains his influence in writing from his studies about the Fraternity as well as his studies in becoming an Episcopal Priest at the University of the South: School of Theology. He continues to dedicate his time to exploring the religious aspects of Masonry and where Christianity plays a role in it.

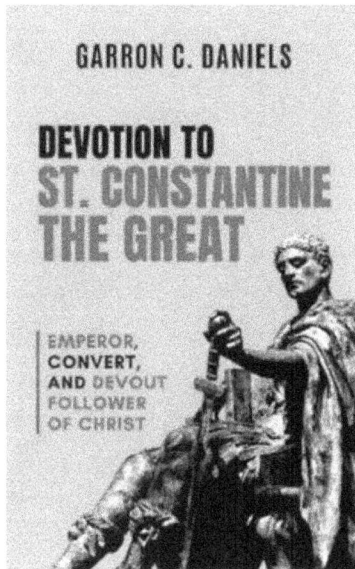

Devotion To St. Constantine the Great:

Emperor, Convert, and Devout Follower of Christ

By Garron C. Daniels

Emperor Constantine the Great is a figure that some throughout history have deemed controversial. Yet, his significance and conversion to Christianity have impacted the faith in ways we will never fully understand. While he was a flawed sinner like any other, he still was the primary force that helped bring Christianity from an oppressed faith to being the religion of the Empire. Constantine was truly a Saintly figure who lived to serve not just as an Emperor but as a mere servant to the Almighty. Because of this, we must seriously and sincerely believe that Emperor Constantine the Great should be considered St Constantine, an emperor, convert, and a devout follower of Christ.

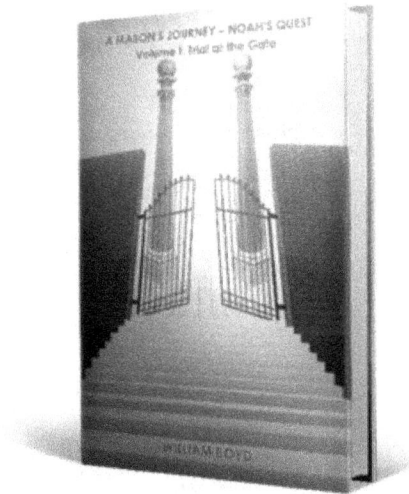

A Masons Journey – Noah's Quest:

Volume I: Trial at the Gate

By William H. Boyd

A Mason's Journey – Noah's Quest" Volume I, Trial at the Gate," is a fictional look at a masonic journey, and it is unusual because it starts at an unexpected point in a mason's journey. It is an introduction to Brother Noah Lewis as he reconciles the books of his life and discovers the unseen forces at work, guiding him along his journey. Above all, it contextualizes and illustrates some of the ideas and concepts the author has believed and have described in a variety of other non-fiction vehicles and may, perhaps, be the first in a series intended to animate the tenets of freemasonry through the fictional quest of Brother Noah Lewis. We all have beliefs about our call to accountability and how we may ultimately learn the value of our labors.

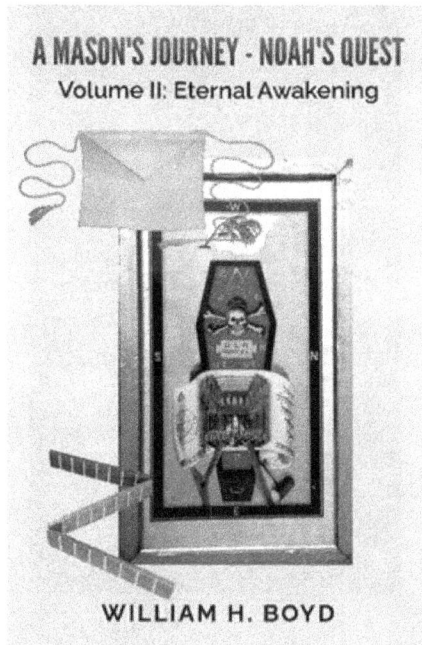

A MASON'S JOURNEY - NOAH'S QUEST
Volume II: Eternal Awakening

WILLIAM H. BOYD

A Masons Journey – Noah's Quest:

Volume II: Eternal Awakening

By William H. Boyd

In book two of the series Noah has come upon The Gate, he had been presented with poignant scenes that were steeped in meaning and were obviously intended to impact him in certain ways. But there was so much he still did not know about this reality and what, if any, control he held. He did not know if or how he should interact with these scenes as they unfolded around him. And he did not know if the scenes were real. Or maybe they were allegories for events from his life gone by? Perhaps they are intended to represent new lessons, meant to teach him further lessons?

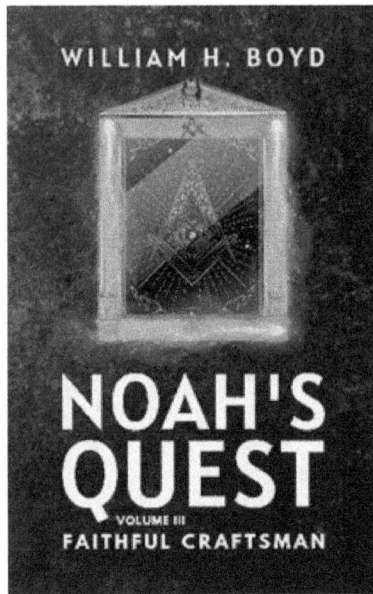

A Masons Journey – Noah's Quest:

Volume III: Faithful Craftsman

By William H. Boyd

Brother Noah Lewis continues the quest begun when he unexpectedly finds himself at The Gate in Volume I: "Trial at the Gate." Since his arrival, he has been tested on his ego and self-awareness in preparation for an entirely new journey on an entirely new path.

In Noah's Quest – Volume III: "Faithful Craftsman," Noah begins to see how all of the pieces of his life and his masonic journey fit together in the larger scheme of life on Earth and in eternity. Noah learns a valuable lesson on the passage of time and the immortality of the soul.

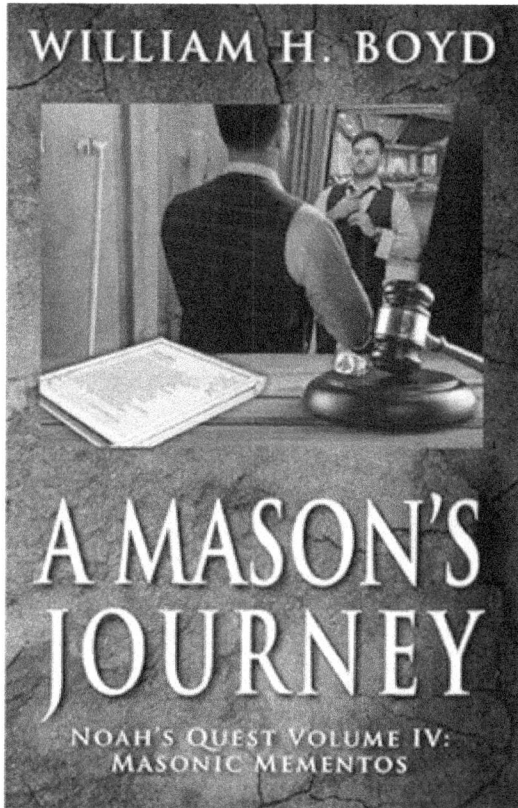

WILLIAM H. BOYD

A MASON'S
JOURNEY

NOAH'S QUEST VOLUME IV:
MASONIC MEMENTOS

A Masons Journey – Noah's Quest:

Volume IV: Masonic Mementos

By William H. Boyd

Noah's Quest is dedicated to my brothers in general and new masons in particular who may be curious or unsure of our masonic boast of "making good men better." I have endeavored through this work to provide my thoughts and insight into how exactly this can happen for any man who may be so inclined and willing to commit to his journey fully.

To those of you who may be starting your masonic journey, I offer this thought – you must actively engage all aspects of masonry to reap the full reward of improvement. It is the internal and not the external qualities that qualify a man to be made a mason; therefore, improvement must begin internally and be rooted in one's heart and one's soul if it is to provide that new, stronger foundation on which we may build our new and improved self, that magnificent edifice that will be seen as worthy of emulation and pleasing to the Grand Architect of the Universe.

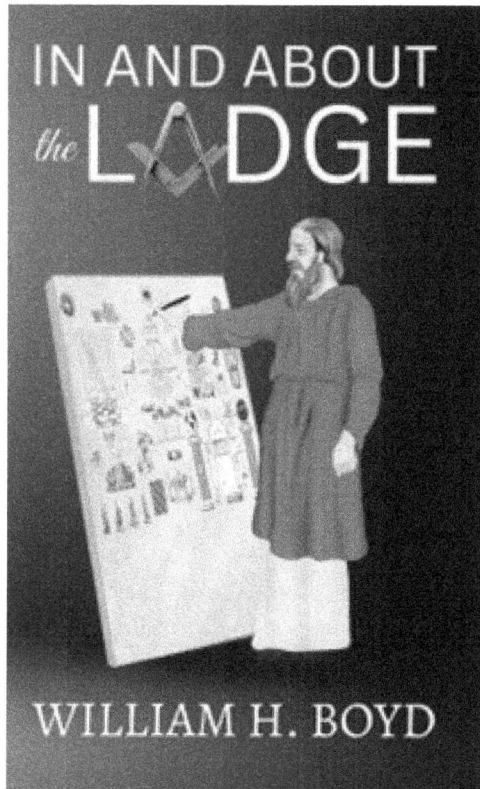

In and About the Lodge

By William H. Boyd

In his second excursion into non-fiction, Brother William H. Boyd explores the lodge's role in the masonic experience. He examines how it supports the Masonic goal of "making good men better." He has assembled a collection of articles and blog posts that address how the lodge experience facilitates a man's quest for improvement. The centerpiece of this collection is a particular article titled "A System Called Masonry," it serves as the foundation upon which the other articles are written and represents the bricks of this allegorical edifice.

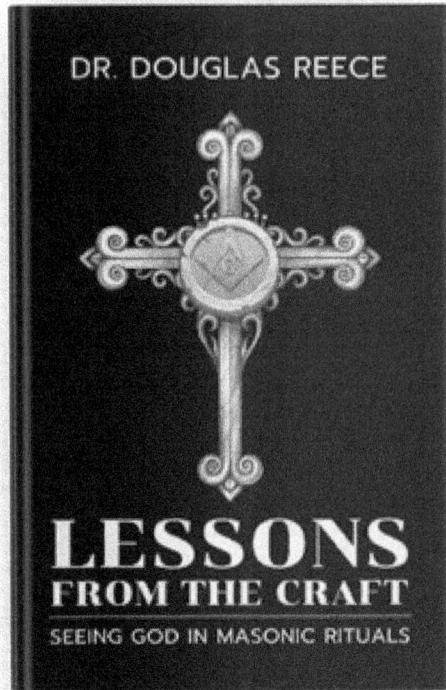

Lessons From the Craft: Seeing God in Masonic Rituals

By Dr. Douglas Reece

Freemasonry has some of the best practical life lessons contained in our ritual ceremonies. The Great Architect of the Universe inspired me to start my ministry and write down within the pages of this book the lessons I have learned for the benefit of the brethren now and in the future. So, with the guidance of the Holy Spirit, I share with you what I have discovered throughout my search for Christ in the Masonic Ritual. May you find within this book lessons, revelations, meanings, and explanations inspiring enough to start your masonic quest for knowledge and meaning.

DR. DOUGLAS REECE

LESSONS
FROM THE RITE
OF ADOPTION
SEEING GOD IN MASONIC RITUALS

Lessons From the Rite of Adoption: Seeing God in Masonic Rituals

By Dr. Douglas Reece

Even the appendant bodies of Freemasonry have beautiful, practical lessons contained within the Holy Scriptures. The pages of this book provide some of those lessons and a brief exploration of seeing Christ in the appendant bodies of The Order of Eastern Star and the Order of Amaranth. May you find the lessons, revelations, meanings, and explanations in these pages inspiring enough to expand your Masonic quest for knowledge and meaning.

The Rite of Adoption consists of the following degrees:

1. The Eastern Star, the first or initiatory degree.

2. The Queen of the South, the second degree.

3. The Amaranth, the third degree.

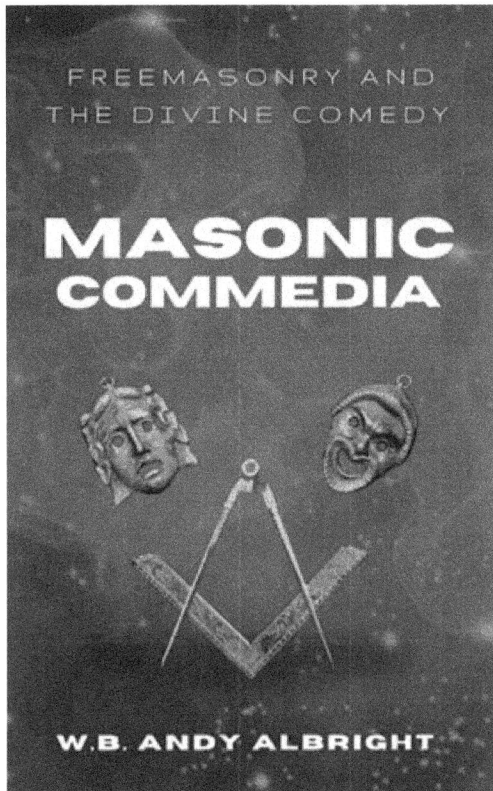

Freemasonry and the Divine Comedy

Masonic Commedia

By W.B. Andy Albright

A well-informed Mason is one who tried to improve himself in Masonry as he knows it, applying our generous principles to our lives. If we learn from the great intellectual ancestors, we improve ourselves tremendously as men and masons. Andy Albright has added to the possibility of improvement through his book "Masonic Comedia: Freemasonry and the Divine Comedy."

In this well-considered book, Albright weaves a set of narratives linking Dante's "Divine Comedy" to masonic teachings in a practical way. If you have not read Dante, you will want to after reading Albright's book but will enter into that achievement well-informed and considering more than the simple story that some get from that monumental work. The faithful reader will also reflect more on the lessons he has learned and how they influence everyday life and thoughts of eternal salvation, regardless of that brother's faith tradition. – R.W.Bro. Robert J.F. Elsner, 33°, KYGCH

Share Freemasonry with Future Generations with These Childrens Books

By

Christophor J. Galloway

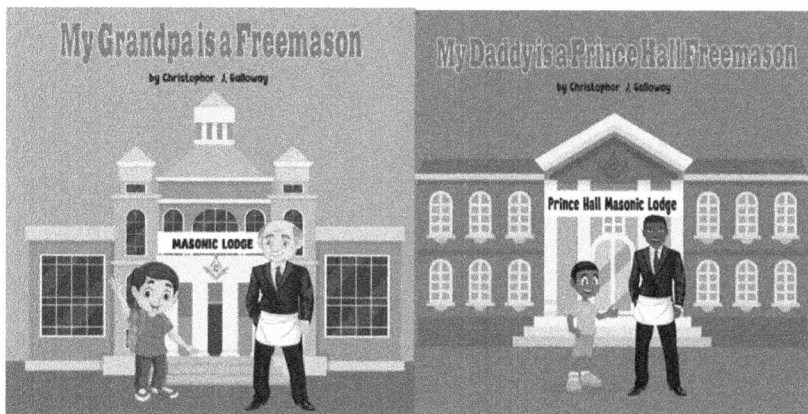

www.ingramcontent.com/pod-product-compliance
Lightning Source LLC
LaVergne TN
LVHW011152080426
835508LV00007B/362